The New Music Therapist's Handbook

Second Edition
Completely Updated and Revised

Suzanne B. Hanser

The New Music Therapist's Handbook
Second Edition, Completely Updated and Revised
by Dr. Suzanne B. Hanser, Ed.D., MT-BC

BERKLEE PRESS
Dave Kusek, Director
Debbie Cavalier, Managing Editor
Ola Frank, Marketing Manager
Jonathan Feist, Senior Writer/Editor
David Franz, Contributing Editor

Cover Design: Moore Moscowitz
Book Design: Dancing Planet MediaWorks™

ISBN 0-643-00645-2

1140 Boylston St.
Boston, MA 02215-3693 USA
(617) 747-2146

Visit Berklee Press Online at:
www.berkleepress.com

DISTRIBUTED BY

HAL•LEONARD®
CORPORATION
7777 W. BLUEMOUND RD. P.O. BOX 13819
MILWAUKEE, WISCONSIN 53213

Visit Hal Leonard Online at:
www.halleonard.com

*To the memory of my parents
and the future of my children*

Contents

Foreword

Eli H. Newberger, M.D.

Techniques of treating various conditions through the use of art and music are showing remarkable success, yet remain mysterious and suspicious to more mainstream health care practitioners. The way that they find acceptance is through clear communications, such as this compelling handbook by Dr. Suzanne Hanser.

Dr. Hanser's mission is fourfold: 1. to define clearly what music therapy has to offer, approaching the task of patient care with seriousness, and rigorous attention to the objectives and methods that usefully address each patient's needs; 2. to gather data that will enable us to measure how we are making a difference in the individual lives; 3. to establish linkages—and to educate our colleagues in other professions—that will lead to more, and more wisely conceived, referrals; and 4. to build the base of support for music therapy as a vital component in the world of health care.

These tasks, Dr. Hanser makes clear, must be undertaken thoughtfully and sensitively. To the extent we are able, we must as well humbly and philosophically come to terms with our own lives, histories, motivations, and human and aesthetic responses. One of the things I love about this book is Dr. Hanser's constant acknowledgement of her own life and how her personal experience motivates and affects her choices and decisions. Courageously, she offers herself as a model of reflective consideration of oneself in relation to one's profession. I think all health care professionals should examine how their work and their own lives fit in a larger human struggle, in the effort to humanize health care.

Nobody would engage in this therapeutic endeavor if they didn't believe in the potential of music to ennoble the experience of life, to connect us meaningfully to others, and to allay the burden of human suffering. It's a professional calling that has a profound origin in our shared knowledge of the transformational power of this art form. We are constantly changed, even as our clients' lives are enhanced, with each performance, with each patient encounter.

Dr. Hanser's emphasis on systematic thought, planning, and evaluation is well taken. This, to me, is the great accomplishment of this handbook. Whatever the romantic appeal of music, and however strong is our belief in its curative value, a careful and scientific approach is required. Accomplishing change is relatively easy. Making sense of it, fitting it in to a larger program of care, weaving in an art to a practice grounded in science, is a much greater challenge. This guide truly shows the aspiring music therapist how to sensibly approach these tasks.

Preface

The New Music Therapist's Handbook is designed for music therapists, allied health professionals and students as a guide to treatment planning. The former edition of this work, the *Music Therapist's Handbook*, has been used as a music therapy text, primarily for advanced methods courses, clinical practica and internships. The current volume applies the same data-based approach to contemporary music therapy practice, expanding the model to include ten stages of treatment planning, from referral to termination.

This new text introduces each stage with personal anecdotes and clinical examples, drawn from my experience as clinician, educator, researcher and mother. I hope that this perspective will enable the reader to apply the principles and guidelines offered in the text to diverse new clinical settings and technological advances. The emphasis on accountability should offer music therapists the tools to document and justify their work at a time when cost-saving measures are taking priority in health care and special education services.

Each chapter includes references, key words, and a bibliography for further reading. The clinical examples are based on true scenarios with adaptations to ensure the confidentiality of each person. As the book guides you through the design, implementation and evaluation of music therapy, you become acquainted with the very special people who are the beneficiaries of the creative and efficacious treatment modality that we use. Music therapy combines the best of art and science in the service of helping others. *The New Music Therapist's Handbook* seeks to guide the process throughout the course of treatment.

Acknowledgements

A book grows from many seeds. The fruits of this book have flowered with the wisdom, talent and energy of many people who help me learn how to sow seeds every day of my life.

As they grow into loving and nurturing people, my children, Leora, Sam, and Raviva, show me what is important in life, and I am in awe.

As I learn with them, my students at Berklee College of Music use their talents to feed the creativity of others, and I am humbled.

As I learn with them, my music therapy colleagues at Berklee College of Music, Colin Lee, Karen Wacks, Julie Buras Zigo and Duane Claussen, teach me new ways that music is therapy.

As we work together in the service of others, my fellow educators, music therapists, clinicians and researchers demonstrate the efficacy of music therapy over and over again.

As I grow as a professional, my mentors, Cliff Madsen, Donald Michel, Doug Greer, Larry Thompson, and Dolores Gallagher-Thompson continue to guide me.

As I strive for the consistency of my words with my beliefs, values, and life experiences, my friends, especially Suzy Conway, Diane Finkel, Robin Stroud, Shira Shore, Laurie Peck, Mitch Benoff, Louise Montello, Barbara Wheeler, Andy Futterman, Amy Wolfson, Peter Alhadeff, Audree O'Connell, Shelley Roth, Rebecca Perricone, John and Sandra Lutzker, and Chad and Amy Furman, support me.

As words create pages and pages create chapters, Donna Chadwick, Samantha Morrow and Elizabeth Driver are skillful editors.

As readers of this text, you have shown an interest in this special field of music therapy and encourage people like me to share my experience with you.

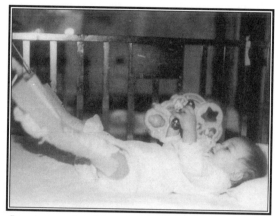

Joy is not in things, it is in us.
—*Richard Wagner (1813–1883)*

Chapter 1

An Introduction to Music Therapy

I am a music therapist. To me, that means that I bring out the creative spirit in everyone I see. I find their music, the part of them that is free, the part of them that sings, the part of them that is rhythm. We all have this music. It shows itself when a song "comes into our heads," or when we tap a toe to music. When we are unable to think or speak or move or be who we once were, we still have this music. It helps us express and communicate. It helps us feel good. It moves us, often deeply, always naturally.

The impact of music on human behavior has been discussed and documented throughout history. The significance of music in both our cultural heritage and our daily lives has been affirmed through countless examples of its power. References to music's universality, magic, and myths confirm the belief that music is a potent human influence. Some have boldly pronounced that music defies the laws of nature, with its "charms to soothe the savage beast, to soften rocks, or bend a knotted oak" (Congreve, 1697). In fact, the claims for its beauty have been so greatly magnified that music is purported to exert supernatural force. The endorsement of writers from ancient healers to Biblical authors has led to a belief that the capabilities of music are mystical and incomprehensible.

Thus, the field of music therapy falls prey to the assertion that the effects of music cannot be explained. To the contrary, much of the impact of a musical experience is observable and measurable. The constituents of a response to music may be isolated, and it is possible to establish a cause and effect relationship between music and behavior. The effects of the "art" of music are, thus, substantiated through scientific methodology.

What guides my work as a music therapist is my own musicianship and an intuitive sense of how music affects the people I serve. They may try a new behavior, focus on a talent or ability, or find a positive force within that allows them to overcome certain limitations or problems. The process is complex. It is also based upon scientific principles, objective observation and systematic assessment of the person's needs.

A considerable body of experimental and clinical research examines the effects of music in its many forms, including performing instrumental and vocal music, listening, composing, improvising, moving to, conducting, analyzing, or talking about, music. The clientele benefiting from music therapy is, likewise, varied, encompassing young and old, acutely and chronically ill, educationally, physically, socially, and emotionally challenged. The settings range from large residential treatment centers for the severely challenged and hospitals to schools, community-based programs and clinics for individuals with specific or short-term problems. As aid is sought for whatever ails people, music therapy demonstrates its ability to help an ever-increasing number of individuals.

Because the scope of music therapy practice is so broad, it is difficult to define the field. Bruscia devotes an entire book to *Defining Music Therapy* (1998). His working definition states: "Music therapy is a systematic process of intervention wherein the therapist helps the client to promote health, using music experiences and the relationships that develop through them as dynamic forces of change" (p. 20). The specialized application of music as therapy will vary depending upon the setting, the therapist, and the selected technique. Even the function of music may be quite different as the music therapist encounters each new clinical problem. Common to every music therapy program is that it applies one of the many forms of music as its primary medium and is based on the needs of the clients it serves.

Music Therapy with Children and Adolescents

Thanks to the Education for All Handicapped Children Act of 1975, Public Law 94–142, children in the United States are provided a free education in their least restrictive environment. As the law is currently implemented under the Individuals with Disabilities Education Act (IDEA), music therapy is mentioned as a Services-Program Option which may be a related service written into a child's *Individualized Education Plan (IEP)*. Children with special needs may be referred for music therapy to meet communication, cognitive, sensory-motor or perceptual-motor, social, emotional, and psychological needs. Music therapists work to remediate skills, change specific behaviors, improve existing conditions, or teach new skills through musical experiences. Adolescents and young adults have an Individualized Program Plan (IPP) to guide their referrals. This document is based on the same format as the IEP and serves the same function for the adult with a disability.

According to "A Descriptive Statistical Profile of the 1998 AMTA (American Music Therapy Association) Membership" (AMTA, 1998) music therapists serve the following children (in order of frequency):

- developmentally disabled
- behaviorally disordered
- emotionally disturbed
- physically disabled
- school age population
  (may be inclusion classes and mainstreamed children or a diverse collection)
- multiply disabled
- speech impaired
- autistic
- visually impaired
- neurologically impaired
  (children and adults)
- hearing impaired
- substance abuse
  (children and adults)

3

- abused or sexually abused
  (children and adults)
- early childhood
- dual diagnosed
  (children and adults)
- head injured
  (children and adults)

Other populations include children with *Rett Syndrome*, AIDS, eating disorders, medical needs, burns, bereavement, *Down's Syndrome*, premature birth and neonatal needs, spinal cord injuries, *Williams Syndrome*. In some cases, non-disabled children also receive music therapy.

Developmental Disabilities

The most frequently served clinical population in children is *developmental disabilities*. This diagnosis refers to disorders which originate during childhood and continue indefinitely, affecting functional abilities substantially. One common developmental disability is *mental retardation*. According to the Diagnostic and Statistical Manual (Fourth Edition) of the American Psychiatric Association (1996), mental retardation appears in mild, moderate, severe and profound forms. For the mentally retarded child, music therapy attempts to create an environment of fun and enjoyment in which those who generally associate learning with failure are able to achieve success. While learning a simple song or finger play, recipients of music therapy are simultaneously improving eye contact, attention span, direction-following, verbal imitation, memory, *fine motor dexterity*, and *auditory discrimination*. These outcomes are typical of goals established for music therapy. By pairing words with tones and sentences with melodies, therapists improve communication through speech and language (Cohen, 1992, 1994; Humphrey, 1980; Madsen, Madsen, & Michel, 1975; Popovici, 1995; Rejto, 1973; Seybold, 1971; Walker, 1972).

The music setting also offers opportunities for mentally retarded children to learn social and motor behavior. They gain self-awareness through movement to music, and social interaction through group music therapy. Musical experimentation and stimulation nurture responsiveness to the surrounding environment in the most profoundly retarded child. The music therapist's goal of "increasing responsiveness to the surrounding environment" may be observed as the child moves to a sound stimulus such as a ringing bell. The therapist might look for turning the head in the direction of the sound, gazing at the bell, reaching for it, grasping it, sounding the bell, and imitating patterns of bell-ringing. Even at this most basic level, awareness is initiated and maintained, preparing the way for the development of more complex skills.

The literature is replete with successful applications of music therapy techniques in recognizing the potential of developmentally disabled persons (Carter, 1982; Dorow, 1982; Graham & Beer, 1980; Jellison, 1996; Madsen, 1981). Even in the most *pervasive developmental disorder*, music therapy enhances functional abilities while simultaneously enriching creative and expressive capacities. Enabling individuals to participate in some way at their own level of competence, a music experience challenges growth through developmental stages using a success–oriented medium.

Music has the advantage of demanding attention that a visual stimulus cannot, because it intrudes immediately through ears that cannot be closed voluntarily. This phenomenon, coupled with the nonthreatening nature of musical exploration and auditory stimulation, may be most applicable for the child with a pervasive disorder or delay. An *autistic* child who has previously shunned human interaction may begin to communicate with a therapist who provides positive music experiences. Clinical improvisation is used extensively to enhance communication and expressivity as well as to develop more interactive social skills in autistic children. Through music therapy, they may encounter their first close relationship with a non-family member.

Behavioral Disorders

The next most frequent population treated by music therapists is children with *behavioral disorders*. These disorders include children with *attention deficit or disruptive behavior disorders* who have problems in social behavior which are extreme enough to interfere with the learning process. The behavioral disorders classification also refers to children who have *conduct disorders, oppositional defiant disorders, hyperactivity,* or other non-specific behavior problems. These children are often referred to music therapy to enhance self-awareness, self-expression, or self-esteem. Active music behavior, such as playing an instrument and singing, necessitates using the voice and body in a clearly structured manner to produce the desired musical product. The child's ability to generate socially appropriate behavior which is incompatible with inappropriate behaviors accounts for further success of music as therapy (Madsen & Wolfe, 1979). While engaged in positive creative efforts, a child often gains self-control and a concrete emotional outlet.

At another level, feelings which are misunderstood or difficult to describe verbally may be experienced through the expressive medium of music. Children may be referred to music therapy in order to assess the nature of their emotions. Asking a child to express a particular feeling by playing an instrument may seem indirect; but, it often reveals a degree of emotional arousal which can be observed and explored. Facial affect, nonverbal behavior or "body language" while performing music offer a nonthreatening starting point for understanding emotions.

Learning Disorders

Learning disorders comprise impairments in specific academic areas. One remediation approach is a music teaching model which works through parallel behaviors in the learning of musical skills. For instance, a child who has difficulty coordinating movements of the right and left side of the body can develop this ability through moving to music, using arms and legs synchronously. Playing increasingly more complex melodies on the piano, with hands separately and then together, can develop such coordination. Visual tracking required in translating written music to the keyboard is similar to the left-to-right eye movement necessary for reading words. The ability to listen to others and respond cooperatively at a precise time with a previously learned musical part is required for participation in a musical ensemble. With the motivation to produce music, children often succeed in mastering musical skills while improving such conceptual correlates. Thus, children with learning disorders may benefit in many ways from the demands of these structured musical experiences.

Music may also provide an opportunity for children to process an auditory stimulus and respond to it appropriately. This *auditory-motor match*, such as a person's answer to a spoken question, can be developed effectively through auditory discrimination training with music. At the extreme, musicians who learn to tune string instruments, recall lengthy melodies, or name the pitches of sounds they hear, show a remarkably finely-tuned set of discriminations.

Motor Skills Disorders

Children who have *motor skills disorders* may be delayed in motor development or display problems in gross or fine motor coordination. They may be referred to music therapy because playing instruments necessitates varying degrees of motor and eye-hand coordination, as well as breath control when playing wind instruments. To dance, one must move in specified ways, integrating various parts of the body in a smooth, rhythmic fashion. Listening to music may involve self-discipline and discrimination skills while the experience evokes images, learned responses (such as clapping along), and individual creative reactions (such as free, improvisational movements). Music therapists also assist in the rehabilitation of more severe *neuromuscular* and skeletal disorders of many types. One technique is to use rhythmic and musical cues for specific movements and for body relaxation.

Communication Disorders

Children with *communication disorders* benefit from music therapy in several ways. Clearly, singing involves speech and language, and more specifically, *auditory memory, pitch-matching*, and fluency. Vocal and wind instrument training provide a creative context for specific exercises which may be used in collaboration with speech therapy. Goals include improvement in articulation, inflection, breathing and pacing of speech.

Nonverbal children are especially good candidates for music therapy. Without the obvious means of communication that most of us use, they need to learn other methods to express themselves. Music therapists are adept at offering augmentative communication and computer-assisted music methods to enable these children to express feelings and thoughts through music.

Sensory Impairments

Children with *sensory impairments* may have problems with vision, hearing or both. Children with *hearing impairments* are aided by the sensory stimulation of music and vibratory rhythmic cues offered in music for speech and body movements. As improbable as it may seem at first, there is considerable clinical evidence of the efficacy of music therapy with children who are deaf. Children who are visually impaired benefit from music therapy when they develop their auditory and musical abilities. Their music therapists also contribute to mobility training when unsure or rigid movements become more fluid and natural through intervention with music.

Physical Challenges

Other *physical challenges* comprise conditions wherein impaired physical development or functioning, including sensory impairments, are sufficiently severe to interfere with normal functioning. When a physically challenged child or adult is referred to music therapy, the objective is often to demonstrate to clients that they are capable of performing or creating music heretofore deemed impossible. By modifying musical instruments and using adaptive music technology, music therapists have shown that the sense of worth may be greatly enhanced in a person who is able to produce pleasant sounds. Music therapists have witnessed the joy of quadriplegics who perform for enthusiastic audiences on specially-adapted guitars and the immense pride of people in wheelchairs who learn to dance by using mobile parts of their bodies.

Certain *physical therapy* manipulation with repetitive movements set to music, yields a cheerful experience, which more closely resembles play than work. Music offers incentive to complete uncomfortable exercises as the client executes the necessary movements more smoothly and rhythmically. Music therapists work collaboratively with physical therapists to develop creative treatment approaches for their clients. *Multiply handicapped* children, likewise, succeed with a creative approach which emphasizes one's abilities and strengths as opposed to the often more obvious disabilities and weaknesses.

Children in Inclusion Classrooms

As a group-oriented intervention, music therapy accommodates different levels and abilities, bringing out the best in every child who participates. Music therapy provides a wonderful opportunity for children with special needs to interact positively with children in the typical classroom as they learn together in *inclusion* classes (Gunsberg, 1988; Hughes, Robbins, McKenzie & Robb, 1990; Humpal, 1991).

Special Applications to Adolescents

The various disorders and conditions described above are generally diagnosed or recognized in childhood, but they also affect adolescents and, in some cases, adults. Many music therapists specialize in adolescence and have expertise in the unique challenges facing individuals at this stage of development. Some work within a family therapy model, helping parents and children communicate about their preferred music and the meaning of that music. Another technique is family improvisation, used as a metaphor for understanding patterns of interpersonal interaction within the family or among peers. Music therapists also assist adolescents in understanding the mechanisms that contribute to such problems as eating disorders by becoming more aware of their emotions through expressive music activities.

Music Therapy with Adults

Medical Conditions

The psychological impact of having a medical condition or illness is often overlooked in the search for a medical treatment. Treatment may call for hospitalization, surgery, or other procedures which tend to provoke anxiety in most people. The emotional reaction to even the most inconsequential sickness, perhaps requiring bed rest alone, may be traumatic for some. For others, illness triggers a full-blown mental disorder. Music therapists have designed procedures for inducing relaxation which both ameliorate the anxiety associated with illness or hospitalization, and divert attention away from pain or discomfort. These techniques have been applied to a wide variety of clinical populations in medicine and dentistry (Froehlich, 1996; Standley, 1986, 1996). Patients have responded well, to the point of over-representing the effects, as in a young woman who exclaimed, "I couldn't have had that baby without music!" (Hanser, Larson, & O'Connell, 1983). Often, the need for medication or restraint is minimized when music therapy is introduced.

Applications in the general hospital are expanding rapidly with the acknowledgement that the connection between mind and body is strong. The impact of psychology on physical illness has been documented, and music therapy procedures have been shown to be efficacious strategies for coping with pain and anxiety. People with chronic illnesses can share meaningful experiences in music therapy groups where emotional responses are drawn out and discussed. Some individuals learn new musical skills and begin to appreciate another dimension of their lives. Others are aroused through more passive musical involvement or introduced to new coping strategies through music-facilitated stress reduction. Dramatic research indicates that comatose patients may begin to respond when background music is provided contingent upon their slightest physical movement (Boyle & Greer, 1983).

Mental Disorders

Mental disorders have been classified by the American Psychiatric Association (1996) as clinical disorders, personality disorders or mental retardation, general medical conditions, and psycho-social and environmental problems. A primary treatment modality is psychotherapy, in which music plays a unique role. Music therapists of a wide variety of philosophical persuasions have applied music successfully to psychotherapeutic techniques (Arnold, 1975; Hadsell, 1974; Madsen, 1981; Maultsby, 1977). They have capitalized on the nonverbal aspects of musical expression as a means of observing, understanding, and changing feelings and emotions (Tyson, 1981; Unkefer, 1990). The music therapy setting becomes a microcosm, eliciting interactive social behavior which may be shaped as therapy progresses. Reactions to and perceptions of music, discussions of musical themes, and problem-solving in a musical context are parallel behaviors for responding to similar situations outside the therapy environment. Dealing with these issues in the supportive and positive music setting can assist the person in tackling the real problems.

Another therapeutic aspect of music is the meaningful content and affect conveyed to the listener through musical compositions. Individuals may begin to understand their own feelings when they listen to a song which expresses similar ideas. A discussion of Simon and Garfunkel's "Bridge Over Troubled Water" may yield new insights into sources of support while it presents options for adjusting to troubling circumstances.

Images evoked by music listening provide increased understanding. *Guided Imagery and Music* (Bonny & Savary, 1973; Bonny, 1994) has been used to promote deep relaxation, a heightened sense of awareness, and what has been reported to be an altered state of consciousness. The therapeutic potential of the vivid images evoked by the combination of musical stimuli and verbal guiding are just beginning to be tapped. Special applications of music therapy extend to such conditions as *posttraumatic stress disorder* and to those who have been victims of abuse and trauma. *Forensic psychiatric* settings also employ music therapists. People who are unable to process painful material find a way to access emotions by engaging in music experiences which bring out spontaneous nonverbal expression. Improvisation, songwriting and lyric analysis are popular music therapy techniques. In all of these instances, the music therapy setting offers a structure within which cognitive, social/emotional and overt behavior may be revealed, examined and changed. Perhaps, herein lies its power.

Correctional Psychiatry

Working with both *juvenile offenders* and adults who are incarcerated in a correctional facility, music therapists play an important role in rehabilitation. The structure provided through music therapy allows offenders to participate in healthy, positive experiences, learning to deal with impulse control, interpersonal dynamics, and self-awareness.

Neurological Rehabilitation

Music therapists work with individuals who have sustained a *traumatic brain injury*, *stroke*, and conditions such as *Huntington's* and *Parkinson's diseases* by assisting in the retraining of lost abilities, aiding the recovery process, and teaching adaptive and coping strategies (Lee, 1989; McIntosh, Brown, Rice, & Thaut, 1997).

Community Music Therapy

As community-based treatment and education become more widespread, music therapists have begun to offer services to people who do not have a diagnosable problem, but wish to cope with the stresses and pain that they experience every day. Others desire to realize their potential and develop their self-awareness or expression through music. Music therapists are well-trained to meet their needs and have developed programs for relaxation and self-actualization (Giles, Cogan, & Cox, 1991).

In addition, there are a number of people with special needs who are interested in learning how to develop their voices or play musical instruments. Individuals with conditions such as *Williams Syndrome* generally have considerable musical ability, and require music lessons from someone like a music therapist who is knowledgeable of their unique learning requirements. This direction in music therapy practice is reflective of the growing interest in recognizing the musical potential in all of us.

Music Therapy with Older Adults

Gerontology is the study of late life and its associated characteristics. Music brings energy and life to many people who approach late life with loss of cognitive or physical functioning, not to mention the loss of loved ones or vocational identity. Feelings of worthlessness and despair are transformed into pride when people are shown that they are still capable of being creative and can learn new skills. Often, too, involvement in musical experience which is reminiscent of a joyous time can be extremely revitalizing (Bright, 1981; Clair, 1996; Hanser & Clair, 1995; Smith & Lipe, 1991). The most withdrawn and confused patients suffering from *dementia* due to *Alzheimer's disease* and related disorders are able to participate actively in music therapy sessions. As music demands reality-oriented behavior in the present without risk of failure, even the most cognitively impaired older adults master musical tasks with enhanced self-respect (Brotons, Koger, & Pickett-Cooper, 1997; Koger, Chapin, & Brotons, 1999).

Too often, older adults are given the message that they have outlived their usefulness. The losses which naturally accompany the aging process contribute to a weakening self-concept. These perceptions may soon be overturned when individuals are given the opportunity to cooperate in a musical endeavor enabling some to perform, some to compose, some to accompany, some to listen, and everyone to employ the highest level of creative potential.

At the End of Life

Music therapy holds a special place in the process of preparing for death. Individuals who are dying find a way to express what they are feeling through choosing music to hear, sing or perform, and by composing songs with the help of the therapist. Families who participate together in music therapy transform this difficult time into an experience of unifying creative expression with their loved one (Lee, 1995; Mandel, 1993; Martin, 1991).

Conclusion

The preceding survey of clinical problems has presented a sampling of music therapy practices for identified needs or disorders. Of considerable challenge to the health care professional, however, is the prevention of such difficulties. No musical vaccine has been, or could ever be found for a particular disease. One wonders if people who listen to a piece of relaxing music at the end of a stressful day, play an instrument as a means of self-expression, or channel excess energy into musical participation in an ensemble are at lower risk for distress.

This overview of music therapy has disclosed only a few of the myriad of effects produced by music. It is significant that the claims regarding the strength of music in affecting behavior are not based merely on the casual observations of a single witness, but rather are backed by wide and varied evidence generated through scientific research. With this foundation, the music therapist proceeds to develop an individualized program for each client or therapy group.

The New Music Therapist's Handbook focuses on the client and helps the therapist decide upon the most appropriate and efficacious methods. It presents a model for music therapy treatment planning with individuals who have such conditions as developmental disabilities, behavioral, learning, motor skills and communication disorders, sensory impairments, physical challenges and illnesses, mental disorders, and geriatric conditions. It also describes applications with people who are dealing with the stresses of ordinary life or coping with the discomforts that all of us encounter at some time in our lives. The book is designed for students and practitioners of music therapy who participate in the development of individualized treatment programs, presenting examples of people who benefit from music therapy services. It steers the therapist through the course of planning, implementation and evaluation, offering clinical practice guidelines and real music therapy cases. This approach borrows from principles of music therapy and the behavioral sciences to demonstrate an objective and "data-based" view of music therapy.

Summary

This introduction to the field of music therapy presents applications to a variety of clinical settings. For children with developmental disabilities, music therapy teaches social, motor, academic and conceptual skills. It offers opportunities for self-expression, self-esteem and self-control for children with behavioral disorders. The acquisition of musical skills in a child with a learning disorder brings parallel developments in perceptual-motor and cognitive areas. The positive, creative aspects of music learning offer incentives for freer movement, rhythmic understanding, and enhanced sense of worth in children with motor skills disorders. The melodic and rhythmic elements of speech are enhanced in individuals with communication disorders, and people who are unable to use speech learn new ways to express themselves. Children with sensory impairments or physical challenges develop their talents and strengths through music therapy. Medical patients divert attention from pain while attempting to deal with their illnesses. People with mental disorders respond to the nonverbal metaphor established in the music therapy setting. Geriatric patients become involved in a creative reality-oriented experience which may be revitalizing and reminiscent of joyous times. These populations represent one segment of the clientele who can benefit from the use of music therapy.

Key Words

Alzheimer's disease (dementia of the Alzheimer's type)
>A progressive, degenerative disease with insidious onset, characterized by multiple cognitive deficits and significant decline in functioning.

Attention deficit disorder
>A disorder characterized by maladaptive inattention, hyperactivity, or impulsiveness which results in pervasive and clinically significant impairment. Some symptoms should have presented before seven years of age, although it may be diagnosed in adulthood.

Auditory discrimination
>The ability to hear similarities and differences between sounds.

Auditory memory
>The ability to retain and recall that which is heard.

Auditory-motor match
>The process whereby awareness of sound results in a movement or response.

Autistic
>An individual with autistic disorder, beginning in infancy, which is characterized by self-absorption, preoccupation with inanimate objects, and/or dysfunctional, destructive or ritualistic behaviors.

Individuals who display these characteristics later in life are also sometimes diagnosed as autistic. Autistic disorder is a type of pervasive developmental disorder.

Behavioral disorder
A problem in social behavior which is sufficiently extreme as to interfere with the learning process.

Cerebral palsy
A series of disorders characterized by problems in movement, posture, and loss of voluntary muscle control, which are caused by brain injury early in life.

Communication disorder
A disability which is characterized by the inability to transfer thought through speech, written word or bodily gestures.

Conduct disorder
A persistent pattern of behavior characterized by the breaking of social norms, including serious violations, aggression, destruction or deceitfulness.

Dementia
A set of symptoms characterized by deterioration in cognitive functioning, particularly memory, abstract thinking, judgment and problem solving.

Developmental disability
A disorder originating before the age of 18 which constitutes a substantial handicap and continues indefinitely. The disabilities include mental retardation, autism, epilepsy, cerebral palsy and severe learning disabilities if the origins are related to mental retardation.

Disruptive behavior disorder
A type of conduct disorder characterized by oppositional and defiant behavior which does not meet criteria for other conduct disorders.

Down's Syndrome
A congenital abnormality of the trisomy 21 gene (an extra chromosome), resulting in mental retardation and physical abnormalities.

Fine motor dexterity (coordination)
The use of small muscles for reaching, grasping and manipulating objects.

Forensic psychiatry
The branch of psychiatry devoted to legal problems and infractions of law, primarily criminal.

Gerontology
The study of aging, characteristic behaviors of older adults, and disorders associated with the late life.

Guided Imagery and Music
A technique which involves listening to music in a relaxed state, to elicit imagery, symbols and/or feelings for the purpose of creativity, therapeutic intervention, self understanding and spiritual experience.

Hearing impairment
A global term for any degree or type of hearing loss, including deafness and hard of hearing.

Huntington's disease (chorea)
An inherited disorder, affecting the central nervous system and causing involuntary movements and contortions; may also cause cognitive decline and behavioral symptoms.

Hyperactivity
Behavior which is characterized by increased or excessive muscular activity.

Inclusion
The concept referring to placing children with special needs in the classroom that they would normally attend, and importing support and prescribed related services to that classroom.

Individualized Education Plan (IEP)
A written plan of instruction for each child with special needs, which includes statements of present functioning, long- and short-term goals and objectives, required services and related information. Every handicapped child must have an IEP specifying special education and related services where appropriate, according to Public Law

94–142, the Education for the Handicapped Act.

Juvenile offenders
Children who have committed offenses, according to law.

Learning disorder
A deficit in a specific area related to the processing of input, i.e., learning, resulting in decreased achievement when compared to the norm; often associated with perceptual-motor deficiencies or brain damage.

Mental retardation
Sub average intellectual functioning and impaired adaptive functioning whose onset is during the developmental period; presently, a person with an IQ of 70 or below.

Motor skills disorder
A deficit in coordination, diagnosed in childhood, resulting in significant functional loss, not due to a medical condition and failing to meet criteria for a pervasive developmental disorder.

Multiply handicapped
An individual with more than one diagnosed impairment; a physical or sensory handicap accompanied by another handicap which inhibits normal development or adjustment.

Neuromuscular disorder
A condition affecting the nervous system and the muscles of the body.

Oppositional defiant disorder
A condition characterized by persistent hostile and negative behavior, causing functional difficulties.

Parkinson's disease
A chronic nervous system disorder characterized by tremor, rigidity, and slow movements.

Pervasive developmental disorder (PDD)
A set of conditions, including autism, Rett Syndrome, Asperger's disorder, childhood disintegrative disorder and others. PDD is a relative term for a variety of mental and/or behavioral disorders

without biological cause.

Physical challenges (physical impairment)
A broad term for any impairment of the body which affects functional capacity.

Physical therapy (physiotherapy)
A rehabilitative treatment of physical impairment or challenge, using techniques such as massage, hydrotherapy, heat, and exercise.

Pitch-matching
Imitation of highness or lowness of a sound.

Posttraumatic stress disorder
A type of anxiety disorder in which the person re-experiences a trauma with persistent arousal and avoidance of stimuli associated with the trauma; causes significant distress and functional impairment.

Rett Syndrome
A disorder in which a child with normal early development loses manual dexterity, coordinated gait, social engagement, and language; associated with severe psychomotor retardation and deceleration of head growth.

Sensory impairment
A disorder affecting contact with the environment through the senses (hearing, vision, taste, touch, kinesthesia).

Stroke (apoplexy)
Blockage of the blood supply to the brain which may be transient and temporary, or severe, resulting in paralysis, aphasia (a speech disorder), or incontinence (loss of bowel control).

Traumatic brain injury
A broad term for head injury sustained in an accident or other sudden onset.

Williams Syndrome
A neurobehavioral congenital disorder characterized by delayed motor development, mild to moderate mental retardation and notable impairment in visual and spatial functioning. Children

display hyperacusis, responsiveness to music, and a social and verbal fluency.

References

American Music Therapy Association. (1998). *AMTA Member Sourcebook*. Silver Spring, MD: Author.

American Psychiatric Association. (1996). *Diagnostic and statistical manual of mental disorders* (4th ed.). Washington, DC: Author.

Arnold, M. (1975). Music therapy in a transactional analysis setting. *Journal of Music Therapy, 12*, 104–120.

Bonny, H .L. (1994). Twenty-one years later: A GIM update. *Music Therapy Perspectives, 12*, 70–74.

Bonny, H. L, & Savary, L. M. (1973). *Music and your mind: Listening with a new consciousness*. New York: Harper & Row.

Boyle, M. E., & Greer, R. D. (1983). Operant procedures and the comatose patient. *Journal of Applied Behavior Analysis, 16*, 3–12.

Bright, R. (1981). *Music in geriatric care*. New York: Musicgraphics.

Brotons, M., Koger, S. M., & Pickett-Cooper, P. (1997). Music and dementias: A review of literature. *Journal of Music Therapy, 34*, 204–245.

Bruscia, K. E. (1998). *Defining music therapy*. Gilsum, NH: Barcelona.

Carter, S. A. (1982). Music therapy for handicapped children: Mentally retarded. In W.B. Lathom & C.T. Eagle, Jr. (Eds.), *Project Music monograph series*. Washington, DC: National Association for Music Therapy.

Clair, A. A. (1996). *Therapeutic uses of music with older adults*. Baltimore: Health Professions.

Cohen, N. S. (1992). The effect of singing instruction on the speech productions of neurologically impaired persons. *Journal of Music Therapy, 29*, 87–102.

Cohen, N. S. (1994). Speech and song: Implications for therapy. *Music Therapy Perspectives, 12,* 8–14.

Congreve, W. (1697). *The Mourning Bride.*

Dorow, L. G. (1982). *Music therapy with the mentally retarded: Data-based techniques from 1970–1980.* Washington, DC: National Association for Music Therapy.

Froehlich, M. A. (1996). *Music therapy with hospitalized children.* Cherry Hill, NJ: Jeffrey Books.

Giles, M. M., Cogan, D., & Cox, C. (1991). A music and art program to promote emotional health in elementary school children. *Journal of Music Therapy, 28,* 135–148.

Graham, R. M., & Beer, A. S. (1980). *Teaching music to the exceptional child: A handbook for mainstreaming.* Englewood Cliffs, NJ: Prentice-Hall.

Gunsberg, A. (1988). Improvised music play: A strategy for fostering social play between developmentally delayed and nondelayed preschool children. *Journal of Music Therapy, 25,* 178–191.

Hadsell, N. (1974). A sociological theory and approach to music therapy with adult psychiatric patients. *Journal of Music Therapy, 11,* 113–124.

Hanser, S. B., & Clair, A. A. (1995). Retrieving the losses of Alzheimer's disease for patients and care-givers with the aid of music. In T. Wigram, B. Saperston, & R. West (Eds.). *The art and science of music therapy: A handbook.* Chur, Switzerland: Harwood Academic.

Hanser, S. B., Larson, S. C., & O'Connell, A. S. (1983). The effect of music on relaxation of expectant mothers during labor. *Journal of Music Therapy, 20,* 50–58.

Hughes, J. E., Robbins, B. J., McKenzie, B. A., & Robb, S. S. (1990). Integrating exceptional and nonexceptional young children through music play: A pilot program. *Journal of Music Therapy, 8,* 52–56.

Humpal, M. (1991). The effects of an integrated early childhood music program on social interaction among children with handicaps and their typical peers. *Journal of Music Therapy, 28,* 161–177.

Humphrey, T. (1980). The effect of music ear training upon the auditory discrimination abilities of trainable mentally retarded adults. *Journal of Music Therapy, 17,* 70–74.

Jellison, J. A. (1996). A content analysis of music research with disabled children and youth (1975–1993): Applications in special education. In C.E. Furman (Ed.), *Effectiveness of music therapy procedures: Documentation of research and clinical practice* (2nd ed.) Silver Spring, MD: National Association for Music Therapy.

Koger, S. M., Chapin, K., & Brotons, M. (1999). Is music therapy an effective intervention for dementia? A meta-analytical review of literature. *Journal of Music Therapy, 36,* 2–15.

Lee, C. A. (Ed.). (1995). *Lonely waters.* Oxford: Sobell Publications.

Lee, M. H. (Ed.). (1989). *Rehabilitation, music, and human well-being.* Saint Louis: MMB Music.

Madsen, C. K. (1981). *Music therapy: A behavioral guide for the mentally retarded..* Washington, DC: National Association for Music Therapy.

Madsen, C. K., Madsen, C. H., Jr., & Michel, D. E. (1975). The use of music stimuli in teaching language discrimination. In C. K. Madsen, R. D. Greer, & C. H. Madsen, Jr. (Eds.), *Research in music behavior: Modifying music behavior in the classroom.* New York: Teacher's College.

Madsen, C. K., & Wolfe, D. E. (1979). The effects of interrupted music and incompatible responses on bodily movement and music attentiveness. *Journal of Music Therapy, 16,* 17–30.

Mandel, S. E. (1993). The role of the music therapist on the hospice/palliative care team. *Journal of Palliative Care, 9,* 37–39.

Martin, J. A. (Ed.). (1991). *The next step forward: Music therapy with the terminally ill*. Bronx, NY: Calvary Hospital.

Maultsby, M. C. (1977). Combining music therapy and rational behavior therapy. *Journal of Music Therapy, 14*, 89–97.

McIntosh, G. C., Brown, S. H., Rice, R. R., & Thaut, M. (1997). Rhythmic auditory-motor facilitation of gait patterns in patients with Parkinson's disease. *Journal of Neurology, Neurosurgery and Psychiatry, 62*, 22–26.

Popovici, M. (1995). Melodic intonation therapy in the verbal decoding of aphasics. *Romanian Journal of Psychiatry, 33*, 57–97.

Rejto, A. (1973). Music as an aid in the remediation of learning disabilities. *Journal of Learning Disabilities, 6*, 286–295.

Seybold, C. (1971). The value and use of music activities in the treatment of speech delayed children. *Journal of Music Therapy, 8*, 102–110.

Smith, D. L., & Lipe, A. W. (1991). Music therapy practices in gerontology. *Journal of Music Therapy, 28*, 193–210.

Standley, J. M. (1986). Music research in medical/dental treatment: Meta-analysis and clinical applications. *Journal of Music Therapy. 23*, 56–122.

Standley, J. M. (1996). Music research in medical/dental treatment: An update of a prior meta-analysis. In C.E. Furman (Ed.), *Effectiveness of music therapy procedures: Documentation of research and clinical practice* (2nd ed.). Silver Spring, MD: National Association for Music Therapy.

Tyson, F. (1981). *Psychiatric music therapy: Origins and development*. New York: Creative Arts Rehabilitation Center.

Unkefer, R. (1990). *Music therapy in the treatment of adults with mental disorders: Theoretical bases and clinical interventions*. New York: Schirmer Books.

Walker, J. B. (1972). The use of music as an aid in developing functional speech in the institutionalized mentally retarded. *Journal of Music Therapy, 9,* 1–2.

For Further Reading

Alvin, J., & Warwick, A. (1991). *Music therapy for the autistic child.* London: Oxford University Press.

Atterbury, B. W. (1990). *Mainstreaming exceptional learners in music.* Englewood Cliffs, NJ: Prentice-Hall.

Beggs, C. (1988). *Music therapy management and practice.* Port Lambton, Ontario: Rose Leigh.

Benenzon, R. (1982). *Music therapy in child psychosis.* Springfield, IL: Charles C. Thomas.

Benenzon, R. (1997). *Music therapy theory and manual* (2nd ed.). Springfield, IL: Charles C. Thomas.

Birkenshaw-Fleming, L. (1993). *Music for all: Teaching music to people with special needs.* Toronto: Gordon V. Thompson Music.

Bjørkvold, J. (1992). *The muse within.* (W.H. Halverson, Trans.) New York: Harper Collins.

Boxill, E. H. (1985). *Music therapy for the developmentally disabled.* Austin: Pro-Ed.

Davis, W. B., Gfeller, K. E., & Thaut, M. H. (1999). *An introduction to music therapy: Theory and practice* (2nd Ed.). Boston: McGraw Hill.

Eagle, C. T., & Lathom, W. B. (1982). *Project music monograph series.* Washington, DC: National Association for Music Therapy.

Gaston, E. T. (1968). *Music in therapy.* New York: MacMillan.

Katsh, S., & Merle-Fishman, C. (1998). *The music within you.* Gilsum, NH: Barcelona.

Kenny, C. B. (1989). *The field of play: A guide for the theory and practice of music therapy.* Atascadero, CA: Ridgeview.

Kenny, C. B. (1982). *The mythic artery: The magic of music therapy*. Atascadero, CA: Ridgeview.

Krout, R. (1986). *Music therapy in special education: Developing and maintaining social skills necessary for mainstreaming*. St. Louis: MMB Music.

Lathom, W. B. (1980). *The role of music therapy in the education of handicapped children and youth*. Lawrence, KS: National Association for Music Therapy.

Lee, C., & Gilroy, A. (Eds.). (1995). *Art and music: Therapy and research*. New York: Routledge.

Michel, D. E. (1985). *Music therapy: An introduction, including music in special education*. Springfield, IL: Charles C. Thomas.

Nordoff, P., & Robbins, C. (1992). *Music therapy in special education* (2nd ed.). St. Louis: MMB Music.

Nordoff, P., & Robbins, C. (1992). *Therapy in music for handicapped children*. London: Victor Gollancz.

Peters, J. S. (1987). *Music therapy: An introduction*. Springfield, IL: Charles C. Thomas.

Ruud, E. (1995). *Music therapy and its relationship to current treatment theories*. St. Louis: MMB Music.

Ryko, M., & Hewitt, G. (1994). *Last songs: AIDS & the music therapist*. Toronto: Music Therapy Services of Metropolitan Toronto.

Wigram, T., & Heal, M. (Eds.). (1993). *Music therapy in special education*. Bristol, PA: Jessica Kingsley.

Wigram, T., Saperston, B., & West, R. (Eds.). (1995). *The art & science of music therapy: A handbook*. Chur, Switzerland: Harwood Academic.

Wilson, B. L. (Ed.). (1996). *Models of music therapy interventions in school settings: From institution to inclusion*. Silver Spring, MD: National Association for Music Therapy.

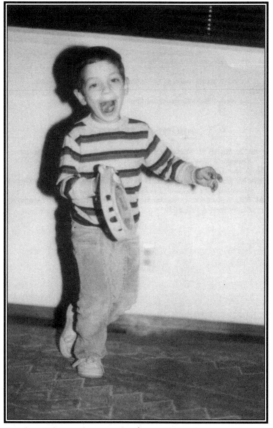

Kids: They dance before they learn there is anything that isn't music.
　　　　　　　　　—William Stafford (1914–1993)

Chapter 2

A Data-Based Model for Music Therapy

I call my approach a *data-based model* for music therapy. The word "data" often conjures up images of computer printouts and massive lists of numerals. I use the term to refer to information obtained through experimentation or direct observation. This data-based model offers guidelines for constructing the most successful treatment program. The music therapist benefits from following these procedures because the effectiveness of a selected technique may be tested throughout treatment. The clients benefit as they observe evidence of their progress in therapy. The partnership between music therapist and client is strengthened as both work together to meet selected *goals* and *objectives*.

I came to develop a respect for data when my daughter, Leora, was born. Because I was an only child who never even baby-sat as a teenager, I had no experience with newborns and panicked at the idea of bringing home a person so tiny and dependent upon me. The parenting literature I studied gave few clues for coping with my infant's cries or understanding her needs. Fortunately, I was blessed to have my friend, Sandra, to teach me about collecting data.

"Data?" my family and friends questioned, shocked to hear me use the word in regard to my dear daughter.

"Yes," I said. "Data collection has helped me understand her primitive language and allowed me to be a better mother."

Let me explain how:

Sandra bought me a notebook which she divided into three sections: feeding, diaper changes, and naps. When I nursed Leora, I was to record the time of day and the number of minutes she nursed. When I changed her diaper, I was to record the time and what I found in her diaper. For naps, I noted each time she fell asleep and woke, calculating the length of her sleep.

Very soon, patterns emerged. She would start crying, and I could see that, for example, she had nursed for a shorter duration at her last feeding, and would probably require more milk at this feeding. I could see that diaper changes were required at a certain interval after feeding. I could begin to plan my schedule around her naps, predicting that she would wake at a particular time, replicating her schedule on the day before. When her schedule began to defy my predictions, by changing drastically, I correctly foresaw a medical problem, and her pediatrician diagnosed an early stage infection.

I actually used a stopwatch to time Leora's nursing, prompting the disdain of my family.

"How can you approach your own child in such a cold and calculating manner?" they asked.

I responded that I loved her too much to leave these important details of her care to chance. By learning her routine, I was not only in better control of our interaction, but I became more confident and relaxed as a mother. I devoted more of my energy to our play, getting to know her through singing, talking, touching, moving and loving her every moment.

At the writing of the new edition of this book, I have been a mother and a music therapist for many years. I have developed my musical talent through study, practice and performance. I have learned new techniques and become more adept at implementing them while maintaining my primary attention on the people I am serving. I believe that my greatest successes, both personal and professional, have involved my being true to the client-centered and data-based nature of my approach. Rather than presenting music therapy techniques in this book, I offer guidelines for determining the client's needs and the framework for the treatment process. The model herein is prescriptive, not by providing a list of music or music therapy techniques for particular problems, but by asking the music therapist to use creativity, experience and personal values to determine the most appropriate goals and techniques.

Stages of a Data-Based Model

This handbook covers ten stages which occur generally in the following order, but which are revisited by the therapist throughout the course of therapy:

1. Referral to Music Therapy
2. A First Session: Building Rapport
3. Assessment
4. Goals, Objectives and Target Behaviors
5. Observation
6. Music Therapy Strategies
7. The Music Therapy Treatment Plan
8. Implementation
9. Evaluation
10. Termination

1. Referral to Music Therapy

The first major step taken in a treatment program is to obtain a referral. The criteria for referral articulate who should be referred to music therapy and for what reasons. There are many unique aspects of music therapy which attract individuals who have not responded to other traditional treatment modalities. Once the referral is made, the presenting problem is identified and translated into an overall goal for therapy.

2. A First Session: Building Rapport

The therapist holds a first session and begins to build the rapport essential for a successful therapeutic relationship. Through observation, more information is gathered about the problem for which therapy is sought. The therapist becomes acquainted with the client, showing interest and genuineness which helps establish trust. A mutually agreeable contract sets the stage for a good working relationship.

3. Assessment

Assessment reveals more about the nature of the problem itself. It determines what the client can or cannot do, knows or does not know. Assessment may involve administering standardized or original tests or observing behavior. It identifies the strengths and weaknesses of the person. A unique feature of music therapy is the assessment of music behavior in addition to non-music behavior. These efforts to quantify behavior in objective terms are performed prior to planning music therapy treatment. However, assessment is an ongoing process which not only helps the therapist determine where to start, but also the direction of therapy, and its expected outcomes.

4. Goals, Objectives and Target Behaviors

The music therapist re-examines the overall goal. When music therapy is successful, this goal will be met. The therapist sets specific objectives along the way to reaching each treatment goal. By defining exactly how that objective will be measured, it is clear when objectives are reached. *Target behaviors* are defined to facilitate the observation of these behaviors throughout treatment.

5. Observation

Observation is one of the therapist's most valuable assessment tools. Several methods of recording allow the music therapist to observe target behaviors to determine their level at the start of therapy and compare this baseline to subsequent changes. Frequency, duration, interval and Planned Activity Check recording are useful techniques for documenting behavioral change.

6. Music Therapy Strategies

In order to prepare the music therapy treatment plan, a wealth of music therapy strategies need to be considered. In addition to selecting specific music therapy methods to meet specific goals and objectives, the therapist must decide whether individual or group therapy is indicated. The therapist will consider behavioral approaches, music techniques to teach other skills, insight therapy, and other systems of music therapy which have been found to be effective. Critical to any approach is the plan for maintenance and *generalization* of gains achieved in music therapy.

7. The Music Therapy Treatment Plan

The music therapy plan reveals a navigational strategy for the course of therapy. A carefully-sequenced hierarchy of objectives provides a therapeutic road map for the plan, locating behavioral landmarks of progress. With the terminal behavior identifying the destination, a sequence of objectives outlines a successful course for therapy. A design for determining treatment efficacy is also selected at this time.

8. Implementation

As the music therapy plan is carried out, the therapist is well-prepared. However, this does not necessarily preclude additional planning in the form of revisions of objectives, adaptations of techniques, or even redefinition and reassessment of the problem. The therapist records progress on an ongoing basis, considers supervision and professional consultation, and reviews the therapeutic relationship.

9. Evaluation

Evaluation of the success of the music therapy program involves a comprehensive analysis. The results which are gathered are accompanied by conclusions and recommendations for future action in a final report. The music therapist ends the treatment program and begins another by defining new areas for change. Music therapy, as a process for learning, continues.

10. Termination

Sometimes, the end of therapy is pre-determined by the school calendar, the limitations of an insurance policy, or a referring professional's orders. At other times, the person who seeks music therapy wishes to continue indefinitely, just as one might enroll in music classes to achieve one's potential, rather than meet a specific objective. There are specific approaches to *termination* of music therapy which respect the best interests of the person in therapy.

Rationale for a Data-Based Model

I sometimes think that the field of music therapy is one of the best kept secrets around. Because the profession is younger and less well-known than many other established disciplines, the people who make decisions about patient care may not be aware of the potential impact of music therapy. They may not realize that there are music therapists practicing in their communities or that music therapy is a treatment option for individuals with a particular diagnosis. Collecting data about a client's progress will provide evidence of the efficacy of treatment. It directly and objectively documents what is happening in the music therapy session. Here are some examples of what may transpire behind the closed doors of music therapy:

Ten-year-old Simon was referred for music therapy because his teacher found him to be particularly respon-sive to music. He loved to dance and sing to almost any piece of music she played during their free periods at school. Simon was diagnosed with a pervasive develop-mental disorder and showed little interest in classroom activities or academics. He could identify his name and several colors, but he was able to recognize only a few words and numbers by sight. Beyond this, he had few basic skills.

The music therapy group at Simon's school was devel-oped specifically to teach academic skills through music. After one semester of participation, Simon was able to spell his name and 30 additional words by singing them. He counted the numbers one through fifteen consistently by playing along on the xylophone. But, curiously, Simon's report card from the classroom teacher showed no such gains. Apparently, none of this learning transferred directly to the non-musical setting. Although phenomenal progress had been made in music therapy, Simon's achievements remained behind these closed doors and the benefits of this new learning did not leak out.

Claude is a 44-year-old man who was diagnosed with Major Depressive Disorder. Every night, he experienced extreme agitation while trying desperately to fall asleep. Finally, he would succumb to sleep, only to greet the following morning in a dysphoric state, with lethargy and sadness. This prevented him from getting out of bed and facing the day ahead, initiating a downward spiral in functioning and an escalation in depression.

The music therapist met with Claude for one hour during which time he taught Claude some simple relaxation techniques and played piano music for him. Claude enjoyed the session immensely. He felt deeply relaxed during both the relaxation alone and the music listening, and he engaged in animated conversation with the therapist as they discussed how his feelings changed. The therapist gave him some cassette tapes to play prior to going to sleep, and suggested that he practice the relaxation techniques. After two days, Claude had complied easily with the instructions and reported instant success in falling asleep. He thanked the therapist for "saving his life," as he put it. He also stated that he no longer required music therapy now that he was able to fall asleep using the techniques on his own.

But, this seemingly "easy fix" now made the therapist skeptical. First of all, was it the music, the relaxation training or the therapist which made the difference? Secondly, would the effects last? Thirdly, had they agreed to meet regularly or was it only the therapist's assumption that they would meet beyond one session? The music therapist did not even know the name of Claude's psychotherapist who should be informed of his response to the music therapy session.

A highly respected university-affiliated hospital is under new management. With the advent of managed care, new policies result in drastic cost-cutting measures. For many years, patients and families have commented extensively about their favorable music therapy experiences. But, the music therapist has nothing in her files about patient satisfaction. While she has been charting progress notes in individual medical records, she has not submitted documentation for any one patient through the course of treatment. When the hospital's new Clinical Director summons the music therapist to his office, the therapist has little to show in support of treatment efficacy. While she is known to her colleagues as an excellent therapist, she finds no way to communicate the impact of what she has done as a music therapist in this hospital. By failing to provide ongoing documentation, the therapist has jeopardized her job and her department.

In each of these cases, music therapy may be considered successful. But, something important is missing. While many positive changes are happening in the music therapy context, there is either a lack of *generalization*, communication, or documentation of these effects. Simon's music therapist has failed to recognize that he has not transferred the educational gains achieved in music therapy to the classroom. Simon reaps limited benefit from music therapy and does not build upon the learning that has taken place. Claude did not contract with the therapist to determine either the objectives of treatment or a method of communication with other professionals caring for him. The people who care about or care for Claude are not properly informed about the positive outcomes of music therapy and cannot integrate these successful techniques into their own efforts to help him. The music therapist is still left with questions about the role of music in helping Claude sleep and the long term effects of this intervention. In the unfortunate case of the hospital music therapy department, an entire program may be sacrificed.

Administrators who are in a position to hire music therapists and professionals who consider referring their clients to music therapy often ask, "What does music therapy seek to accomplish?" "How effective is it in meeting its goals?" "Do the benefits of music therapy services justify their costs?" (Bergen & Strupp, 1972; Briar, 1973). These inquiries are important to every profession which seeks to be accountable to others. *Accountability* refers not only to a profession's self-analysis, but also to its being "answerable and responsible for mutually agreed upon obligations to its constituencies, (clients, community groups, and funding bodies)" (Rust, 1979). For music therapists, accountability means describing the processes which affect the people with whom they work and providing objective evidence of their effectiveness. By further communicating these ideas to clients, colleagues, legislative agents or others, music therapists establish the basic parameters of their task.

With accountability, comes the responsibility to help the client. Once a therapeutic relationship is established with a client, it is difficult, if not undesirable, to be detached and objective. The therapist strives to develop *empathy* and *insight*, characteristics which, by their nature, call for subjective analysis and evaluation of client behavior. Thus, with accountability, comes a classic dilemma.

Techniques exist for introducing objective evaluation into the subjective therapeutic relationship without cross-interference. One such method involves the establishment of expected therapeutic outcomes in identifiable, behavioral terms. These outcomes are defined first in terms of goals which describe the overall purpose or intent of therapeutic intervention. Later, the therapist articulates specific behavioral objectives. These objectives delineate the behaviors around which music therapy will focus, and define when and how much they are expected to change. The behaviors of interest are also called *target behaviors*, because the therapist zeroes in on these observable, measurable behaviors and shoots for a defined change. The therapist who fails to define objectives may be open to other interpretations of success, and held accountable for behavioral change or lack of it in areas other than those treated by the music therapist. For example, such a problem arises when the music therapist teaches the client how to play guitar in order to improve self-esteem, but the client's expectation (objective) is to be able to perform professionally.

Also, consider the case of a young woman who is identifying and expressing aggressive feelings as a function of listening to and discussing musical recordings in the therapy session. The therapist believes that this is an indication of progress. However, when the client subsequently gets angry at family members, the effects of the session are not viewed as ameliorative by either her family or other counselors. This example points out the importance of developing objectives through team consensus, and contracting with the client to work toward these ends.

Only after objectives are set, defined, and agreed upon can therapy be planned, implemented and evaluated effectively. The music therapy plan, obviously, should have the highest probability of success. To ensure this, the therapist may consider such questions as, "Is there evidence that the selected music therapy methodology has been effective in similar cases?" and "How will the therapist determine treatment efficacy?" Evaluation is sometimes difficult, especially since each moment of music therapy may bring a new synthesis of music, technique and therapist. But, evaluation is possible and necessary to maintain accountability for one's own behavior as therapist as well as for therapeutic change in the people being served. Finally, when the goal is reached, termination is considered. The accumulated data will support or refute this decision in ways that the therapist, client and team can understand. The data-based model for music therapy attempts to provide answers to the many questions asked of the therapist and the music therapy profession as a whole. Like any scientific analysis, it will elicit more questions than answers regarding the potential of music as therapy.

Summary

The data-based model concentrates on how to make decisions regarding the client's needs and how to plan, implement, evaluate and terminate treatment. The ten stages of the model are introduced: Referral to Music Therapy; A First Session: Building Rapport; Assessment; Goals, Objectives and Target Behaviors; Observation; Music Therapy Strategies; The Music Therapy Treatment Plan; Implementation; Evaluation; and Termination.

The rationale for using this approach is based primarily on the need for accountability. The model provides a systematic way to structure music therapy experiences and meet treatment goals in an efficient manner.

Key Words

Accountability
The process by which one is responsible and answerable for obligations to a set of constituencies.

Assessment
A systematic approach to the evaluation, appraisal or observation of a person's strengths and weaknesses in preparation for treatment planning.

Data-based model
An approach based on information retrieved through experimentation or direct observation.

Dysphoric
Having feelings of dejection, misery, and underestimation of self.

Empathy
The sense of understanding another person's feelings, ideas and desires by placing oneself into the other's frame of reference.

Generalization
The process of transferring or applying responses to a different set of stimuli, new setting or another behavior.

Goal
Expected therapeutic outcome; a purpose or direction for therapy.

Insight
The self-knowledge and deep understanding of personal issues, primarily regarding the dynamics and roots of symptoms.

Objective
An expected outcome of therapy which defines the goal in clearly observable and measurable behaviors.

Target behavior
A behavior or set of behaviors which provide the focus of therapy identified in the therapeutic goal or behavioral objective.

Termination
    The final stage of therapy which should include
    evaluation of progress, a plan for phasing out and/or
    ending therapy, recommendations for the future
    and a follow-up plan.

References

Bergen, A., & Strupp, H. (1972). *Changing frontiers in the science of psychotherapy*. Chicago: Aldine-Atherton.

Briar, S. (1973). The age of accountability. *Social Work. 18,* 114.

Rust, M. A. (1979). A community mental health accountability scale. *Journal of Community Psychology, 7,* 328.

For Further Reading

Hanser, S. B. (1980). *Music therapy practicum: A manual for behavior change through music therapy*. Oakland: Pea Press.

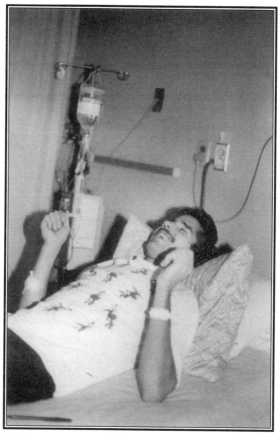

Without music, life would be an error.
　　　　　　—*Friedrich Nietzsche, 1888*

Chapter 3

Referral to Music Therapy

When I was a young girl, I should have been referred to a music therapist. For many years, I ran a low-grade fever and had little appetite. My parents took me to specialist after specialist, whose invasive examinations frightened me beyond words. I was hospitalized repeatedly for exploratory procedures and surgeries, never knowing what would happen next and how much it would hurt.

Finally diagnosed with a congenitally deformed bladder, I had major reconstructive surgery which required a lengthy recuperative period of bed rest. During the many months at home, I was isolated and fearful about my recovery. The physicians and nurses pronounced me a "good girl." I was always extremely cooperative, and rarely screamed out or cried. I had been traumatized by the pain of repeated medical interventions and surgeries. Not surprisingly, I was slow to recover.

My piano became my best friend. When I played the instrument, I felt whole and alive. My mother said that she could tell my mood by how I played. Of course! I could express every nuance of my hidden feelings while interpreting my favorite composers. At the piano, I was healthy.

This experience led me to seek out and pursue the profession of music therapy for my life's work. When I needed it most for my own well-being, however, music therapy was relatively unknown. Neither my parents nor my physicians were familiar with this form of treatment, and there were no music therapists employed at the hospital. Now having reviewed my own history, I realize what a strong candidate I was for music therapy, and wonder how much of my physical and emotional pain might have been reduced with the intervention of a music therapist.

The profession of music therapy has evolved significantly since that time. A growing number of health service providers are aware of its potential and now are referring their clients to music therapy. This chapter samples just a few of the people who become beneficiaries of music therapy, describes the presenting problems which brings them to this special service, and addresses the goals which their therapists establish for their treatments.

The Referral Process

Candidates for Music Therapy

Lorne was diagnosed with Williams Syndrome, a genetic condition which leads to mild or moderate developmental delays, specific medical symptoms, and hyperacusis. This latter symptom is an extreme sensitivity to sound which is also associated with a responsiveness to music and an ability to make very fine auditory discriminations. In Lorne's case, he spends most of his free time on the keyboard where he loves to pick out familiar melodies and improvise. He was referred to music therapy by his parents who believed that music could capture his attention and teach him other skills.

Frieda was referred by her physician. She had been diagnosed one year ago with fibromyalgia. Unfortunately, many pain medications were contra-indicated for Frieda because she also suffered from hypertension and diabetes. She felt as though she was too nervous for meditation and she had not responded to other relaxation techniques. Her physician was aware that music and music therapy strategies were often effective distracters from pain. He contacted the American Music Therapy Association for names of local therapists and made the referral.

Alicia was referred to music therapy after the care team of a skilled nursing facility met to evaluate her case. A 78-year-old woman diagnosed with probable Alzheimer's disease, Alicia had been withdrawn and isolated. She also displayed great confusion and agitation, typical of the middle to late stages of the disease. The team had witnessed many cases where music therapy was instrumental in changing mood and improving socialization. For many residents with dementia, music therapy was the most effective way to improve the quality of life.

Referral Criteria

The cases of Lorne, Frieda, and Alicia display three major reasons to refer individuals to music therapy. Lorne had an obvious interest in and responsiveness to music. Frieda is someone who did not benefit from traditional treatments. Alicia's care team believed that her needs could be met best by music therapy techniques which were shown to be effective with people like her.

Music therapy can help almost anyone who is willing to try it. There are no obvious side effects. It is administered individually or in groups, which is often immensely cost-effective. Yet, there are some very important reasons why certain people are particularly good candidates for music therapy. The following are some basic guidelines:

1. When there is strength in auditory learning styles

    Some people learn new subject matter most efficiently when they see visual cues or read written material about it. Others learn better or faster through listening. People in this latter category are sometimes called *auditory learners*. Their strength in the auditory modality may allow them to succeed in tasks which involve responding to verbal instructions or auditory cues.

    It is useful to know the preferred learning style of children who have special needs so that they have a greater opportunity to succeed when approached with new information. Children who display finer abilities in the auditory modality are already more at ease taking in information while listening. They may be particularly good candidates for music therapy.

2. When there is responsiveness to sound or music
It is not necessary to have musical ability or experience to benefit from music therapy. However, people who enjoy music may be predisposed to use it as therapy.

Some people are exposed to a song once or a few times, and are able to recall the words. They may be able to precisely hum a melody they heard recently. They are particularly responsive to music. Sometimes, children who show little awareness of their environment demonstrate a propensity towards musical expression. They may hear jingles on radio or television and sing them back although they are unable to articulate simple speech. At the other end of the life cycle, older adults with dementia may perform music, demonstrating a preserved ability even when they are disoriented in time and place. These individuals are demonstrating through this behavior that music provides a channel to reach them and to develop their hidden potential.

3. When there is physical inactivity or limited mobility
Persons with severe physical impairments or illnesses may only be able to participate in therapeutic approaches which are more passive or *palliative*. Music therapy may be administered at the bedside without disturbing the individual. Passive music listening is noninvasive, but yields an active inner world of associations and images which may be dealt with and processed. Many music therapy techniques make few demands, allowing the person to respond at a level which is comfortable and natural. For those with the potential to develop mobility and motor skills, graduated exercises with musical instruments facilitate growth in this area.

4. When there is limited cognitive capacity
Individuals who have limited cognitive ability may be restricted in the type of therapies from which they benefit. Music therapy is ideal for people who find verbal therapy unproductive or who cannot participate in therapies which require higher brain function. Some musical experiences activate neural pathways which are distinct from those which are excited during intellectual activity. These experiences generate spontaneous behavior which can then be recognized, shaped, and modified, when appropriate. This is particularly important in children with pervasive developmental disorders and adults with dementia.

5. When confrontive therapies are inadvisable
Music therapy is success-oriented, providing a nonthreatening and safe environment for exploration and change. Its techniques are noninvasive and offer the person opportunities to participate in a failure-free, creative and spontaneous endeavor. Children, adolescents and adults can benefit from an approach which builds on a person's strengths and talents, enhancing a positive self-concept.

6. When compliance is a problem
Many music therapy techniques have an element of fun attached to them. Most people who attend music therapy enjoy it while they reap other benefits. Because it applies methods which focus on the person's abilities and preferences, compliance is easy.

7. When there is difficulty communicating or expressing thoughts, feelings, or ideas
Music therapy is indicated for individuals who cannot express themselves freely. Music offers alternative ways of communicating by augmenting a person's repertory of expressive skills. In music therapy, people learn new ways of making themselves heard through music. They can respond in their own unique way, without concern of being judged

right or wrong. For the individual whose emotional capacity is limited, music therapy taps into a world of feelings which may be accessed immediately and unconditionally.

8. When there is difficulty getting along with others
Music therapy facilitates interaction and is well-suited to group therapy and family therapy. Because people with vastly different abilities can participate successfully in a single musical experience or performance when their roles are carefully prepared, music therapy is recommended for individuals with deficits in social or interpersonal skills. Autistic children have a particular affinity for music and benefit greatly from expressive activities. Children and adults who are reclusive or depressed may be drawn out gently. Music facilitates an atmosphere which is conducive to positive social interaction.

9. When there is limited self-awareness
Because music therapy emphasizes success and attempts to uncover the musical and creative nature of every person, it positively influences self-awareness and self-esteem. Individuals who are more friendly with failure than with success are the beneficiaries of this approach which acquaints people with their confident selves as they develop their potential.

10. When traditional treatments fail or are contra-indicated
Often, a referral is made to music therapy as a last resort when other treatments have failed or are associated with undesirable side effects. It is under these circumstances that music therapy has gained a reputation for serving people who cannot respond to other treatment. As music therapy and other forms of complementary medicine or related services achieve a degree of acceptance within the health sciences and educational institutions, last resort is evolving into first choice.

11. When the evidence shows that music therapy interventions are successful

Formerly considered adjunctive, music therapy is coming into its own as a treatment of choice. As shown in Chapter 1, a body of research is confirming what clinicians have observed in case after case. In 1991, the United States Senate Special Committee on Aging cited evidence of the effects of music in testimony which brought about legislation supporting music therapy with older adults (Special Committee on Aging, 1991). In a publication by the Agency for Health Care Policy and Research (1992), music is listed as a pain management strategy, "effective in reducing mild to moderate pain" (p. 17). Supportive research may be the most significant reason to refer an individual to music therapy.

These eleven points are generic criteria for referral. They are not intended to list all of the potential arguments for referring an individual to music therapy. There are indications and contra-indications for specific music therapy techniques and approaches which the therapist will need to determine in each treatment program.

Possible Contra-Indications

Note that previous history of musical involvement is not listed as an indicator for music therapy. One may reason that high significance of music in a person's life justifies its use as a treatment modality. This is not always the case. In some instances, when musical abilities have been lost, an attempt to retrain or involve the person with music may result in an even greater sense of loss. It has been observed, for example, that some people who were formerly professional musicians have disparate results from rehabilitative efforts using music. For the person who once performed a piece effortlessly, reminders that this level of performance is no longer feasible may elicit grief. These music experiences may be counterproductive to the therapeutic goal when they are met with frustration or other similar feelings. The therapist must be prepared to deal with this possibility and affect a therapeutic outcome which is consistent with the treatment plan. This is not to say that music therapy is contra-indicated for professional musicians. Every case must be examined for its own merits.

At times, hearing impairment prevents an individual from participating fully in music therapy. This is a contra-indication for therapy if a person is straining to hear the music in a relaxation exercise and tension increases. This conspicuous example points to the way in which any expectation which is beyond the person's capacity can place unreasonable demands upon the person and become counterproductive to therapeutic process. It is the therapist's responsibility to ensure that the prerequisite behaviors and skills are met before any music therapy intervention is begun.

Educating Referral Sources

Whether the music therapist is in private practice or on the staff of a large facility, someone other than the music therapist will determine, to some degree, who receives music therapy. This points to the importance of educating potential referral agents. Referral sources need to know who benefits from music therapy and why. They also want to know the predicted clinical outcomes for a particular client. To project these parameters, the therapist begins by examining the most important needs of the referred individual. The therapist communicates the existing research supporting the use of music therapy with similar individuals. The presenting problem is then translated into an overall goal for this person. To do this, let us revisit Lorne, Frieda and Alicia.

Presenting Problems and Goals

Lorne's music therapist met with his parents to discuss their expectations for therapy. The therapist learned that Lorne had visual spatial difficulties typical of children with Williams Syndrome, and that this caused great functional challenges in his finding his way around, according to his parents. The therapist concluded that "improving visual spatial skills" would constitute the primary goal of therapy. Then the therapist set out to assess Lorne's abilities in this domain.

Frieda's physician made this referral specifically to provide a new coping strategy for pain management. Initial discussions revealed that Frieda became incapacitated when in great pain. She would then stay in bed, which not only exacerbated her physical symptoms, but her psychological state as well. The music therapist proposed that one of the most important goals for Frieda's therapy might be "to decrease perceived level of pain and to increase time spent out of bed." Her doctor agreed.

The music therapist participating in the nursing facility team meeting learned that Alicia spent many hours alone in her room. The team set one goal in her care plan—that Alicia "socialize with other residents." The music therapist concurred that not only was this a worthy goal, but that group music therapy was certainly indicated. The therapist invited Alicia to join the group for an assessment the very next day.

In these scenarios, the problems which prompt referral to music therapy are reframed in terms which predict the overall outcomes of music therapy. These goals offer a purpose for therapy as well as a direction. They focus the therapist's attention on the most important area for change or improvement.

Sample Music Therapy Goals

Individuals are referred to music therapy for diverse reasons. They may need to manage problems, modify dysfunctional behaviors, overcome impairments, or cope with illnesses. The music therapist will focus on improving skills and characteristics which will help the person grow and change in a positive direction. Figure 3.1 lists some prospective positive goals for which a person might be referred to music therapy. These include the improvement of behaviors to meet communication, cognitive, educational, physical, psycho-social, emotional, daily living, musical, leisure, vocational, spiritual, and quality of life needs.

NEEDS	SAMPLE GOALS
	To Improve:
Communication	Receptive language
	Expressive language
	Verbal communication
	Nonverbal communication
Cognitive	Rational thinking
	Orientation to time, place, person
	Attention to the task
	Attention to teacher, therapist, parent
Educational	Pre-academic skills
	Academic skills
Physical	Sensory-motor skills
	Sensory integration
	Perceptual-motor skills
	Gross motor coordination
	Fine motor coordination
	Eye-hand coordination
	Adaptation to physical challenge
	Breath control
	Lower blood pressure
	Regular gait
	Deep breathing
	Relaxed muscles
Psycho-social	Self-awareness
	Self-esteem
	Self-concept
	Awareness of environment
	Insight
	Adjustment
	Motivation
	Coping mechanisms

Figure 3.1. Client needs and sample music therapy goals.
(Continued on next page.)

Psycho-social (continued)	Interpersonal interaction Family relationships Cooperation Compliance Self-discipline Impulse control
Emotional	Expressivity Creativity Spontaneity Mood
Daily living	Self-help (eating, toileting, bathing, dressing, etc.) Independence
Musical	Musical ability Musical potential Musical repertoire Freedom to express musically Peak, music experiences
Leisure	Use of free time Leisure time options
Vocational	Productivity Satisfaction
Spiritual	Authenticity Presence
Quality of life	Well-being Self-actualization Personal growth Acceptance

Figure 3.1. (*Continued.*)

Summary

People are referred to music therapy for a variety of problems and needs. But, there are some people who may be particularly good candidates because they are auditory learners, are responsive to sound, have limited cognitive capacity, do not respond to confrontive therapies, fail to comply with other treatments, have difficulty expressing themselves, cannot get along with others, have limited self-awareness, have not benefited from other therapy, or have diagnoses which have been shown to respond well to music therapy. Potential clients may have communication, cognitive, educational, physical, psycho-social, emotional, daily living, musical, leisure, vocational, spiritual, or quality of life needs.

Key Words

Auditory learners
> A colloquial term referring to individuals who tend to learn more easily through auditory means (listening) than through visual means (seeing or reading).

Fibromyalgia
> A nonarticular rheumatic disorder, also known as myofascial pain syndrome; characterized by pain, stiffness and extreme tenderness in the muscles.

Hyperacusis
> An extreme sensitivity to sound which is also associated with a responsiveness to music and an ability to make very fine auditory discriminations.

Palliative
> A treatment which is designed to relieve symptoms rather than cure; applied most often with individuals who have chronic or terminal illnesses.

References

Acute Pain Management Guideline Panel. (1992). *Acute pain management in adults: Operative procedures. Quick reference guide for clinicians.* AHCPR Pub. No. 92-0019. Rockville, MD: Agency for Health Care Policy and Research. Public Health Service, U.S. Department of Health and Human Services.

Special Committee on Aging. (1991). Forever young:
  Music and aging. *Hearing before the Special
  Committee on Aging United States Senate.* (August
  1, 1991). (Serial No. 102-9).

For Further Reading

Beggs, C. (1988). *Music therapy management and practice.* Port Lambton, Canada: Rose Leigh Publishing
  Company.

Behnke, C. A. (1996). A music therapist and sole propri-
  etorship. *Music Therapy Perspectives. 14,* 63-65.

Conant, R. P., & Young, H. E. (1996). CCC Music
  Therapy Center and the current tenor of the music
  therapy profession: The logistics of establishing and
  maintaining a music therapy practice. *Music
  Therapy Perspectives. 14,* 53-58.

Knoll, C. D., Henry, D. J., & Reuer, B. L. (1999). *Music
  works: A professional notebook for music therapists*
  (3rd ed.). Stephenville, TX: Music Works.

Music is in the air—you simply take as much of it as you want.
                                    —Sir Edward Elgar (1857–1934)

Chapter 4

A First Session: Building Rapport

Every time I meet a client for the first time, my heart races. I am excited and I am nervous. It is always a new experience, a new connection, a new dynamic. The music is always different; we will create something new; we will find the music for this moment.

Who is this person? What will I learn this time? It is a new beginning for both of us. Where do I start?

This chapter presents some of the ways to structure the first encounter with a new client to use the time productively and build a healthy therapeutic relationship. This first meeting is an important one for establishing roles and expectations. It can be a time of testing by both parties, person and therapist. The person may test the limits of the therapeutic situation by asking questions, trying out behaviors to determine their acceptability, or provoking a reaction in the therapist. Likewise, the music therapist is testing the person's responses to the music therapy environment and gathering information about what the person brings to therapy.

The first session is a time for beginning the process of gaining trust and rapport, essential elements in effective therapy. The music therapist attempts to establish certain conditions which maximize the opportunity to develop a close working relationship with the person.

In this chapter, Erica, John, and Sophie meet their respective music therapists for the first time. The chapter offers guidelines and suggestions for creating an environment conducive to efficient observation and rapport building.

First Encounters

Four-year-old Erica enters the music therapy studio, accompanied by her parents. She immediately breaks the hand clasp with her mother and rushes to an empty corner of the room. Erica has been diagnosed as having early infantile autism, and usually responds to people by running away from them. As the therapist escorts the parents to a desk in the opposite corner of the large room, he informs them about his contact with the child psychologist who recommended that Erica start music therapy. He describes some of the functions of music therapy and its potential for changing behavior. As the parents are asked to reveal their analysis of the current problem at home, the therapist starts a stopwatch, ready to record the duration of Erica's time in the corner. The parents detail the nature of her autistic behavior and the family's response to it. While the adults discuss her medical and developmental history, Erica remains relatively motionless. Finally, she darts over to an area on the floor where simple percussion instruments have been placed. The therapist stops the watch and comments to the parents on Erica's apparent interest. The stopwatch is reset, and the duration of time spent in the corner is recorded on a form devised for this purpose.

The therapist points out that he has placed different musical instruments and apparatus within six large circles painted on the floor of the studio. Each circle contains one of the following: percussion instruments, an autoharp, stereo speakers softly broadcasting children's folk songs, a set of kazoos, whistles and flutophones, a toy piano, and a large drum. The therapist's form lists each of these areas and provides a column for noting time spent there as well as one for a narrative account of the client's responses in each circle (see Figure 4.1).

Client: Erica Date: September 11		
Musical Stimuli	*Time Spent*	*Behavior*
A. Percussion	5 sec.	random
B. Autoharp	2 min., 30 sec.	calmness, interest and interaction
C. Recorded music		
D. Wind instruments		
E. Piano		
F. Drum		

Figure 4.1. Time spent in activities. Recording form.

After only five seconds of examining percussion instruments, Erica dashes to the autoharp, where she experiments by plucking different strings. For two and one-half minutes, she plucks and listens, plucks and listens, while sitting calmly at the circle's center. The therapist suggests that the threesome slowly approach her. He locates a second autoharp and imitates the pattern plucked by Erica. Sitting on the floor, he slides over ever so gradually into the circle, still repeating Erica's notes. Motioning for the parents to move closer, the therapist introduces new autoharp sounds into the imitative duet. He adds an occasional chord to accompany Erica's music. Softly, he begins singing Erica's name and asks the parents to follow along. Soon, all four are involved in the performance. The therapist passes his autoharp to the mother and guides her hands through a few chord strums. She listens to Erica's melody, accompanies and sings her daughter's name, as father and therapist sing along. In this meaningful musical encounter between music therapist and family, information concerning existing channels of social interaction is being imparted.

John attends the Mental Health Center's Day Treatment Program. He was referred to the center when his employer observed him speaking repeatedly with nonexistent coworkers. He admitted hearing voices and was subject to periodic bouts of confusion. Now, in his first day of group music therapy, John is introduced to the other clients. "It's a New Day," a song composed by the group, is sung as the circle of participants join hands and sway in rhythm. In the final verse, everyone adds an original line to the song, describing something they will do this day to make it better than yesterday. Discussion about the song identifies the feelings behind its content. John shares his awkward-ness about talking with a group of "strangers." Prompted by the therapist, others recall similar feelings when they first entered the group.

A recording of soft music is played as the group prepares for relaxation exercises. After locating areas of tension, everyone is asked to listen to the music and relax isolated parts of the body. As the music comes to an end, the therapist suggests that the group members slowly transfer the focus of their energy from their internal selves to the new participant. He asks the group members to think of something they would like to give to John, not a material gift, but a characteristic or feeling that could help him, based on what they have learned about him. The therapist adds that he would like to give John the confi-dence to share freely in the group. Others contribute encouragement, happiness, peace and similar positive attributes. The therapist suggests that the group find a musical recording that they believe John will like. This will be difficult as they know very little about him. Someone named Susan asks John why he is attending the center. He shrugs and guesses that it is because he needs someone to help him get rid of the voices he hears in his head. Susan jumps up and goes directly to the Beatles' collection. "Here," she directs the therapist, "Play 'A Little Help from My Friends'." As the group listens to the song, John is smiling. He likes the selection very much, and thanks Susan. Questions by the therapist to the group regarding the reason for Susan's choice, John's response, the message of the text, the expectations of friendship, and *the emotions communicated by the music, facilitate a rich interaction among all group members.*

Sophie is an energetic, outgoing, and mature teenager. Traveling by wheelchair is not going to arrest her determination to live independently and find a good job, now that she nears graduation from high school. Sophie's frustration with long hours of boredom at home and difficulty in making friends leads her to seek the assistance of a music therapist. "Tell me about yourself, Sophie," incites a lengthy dissertation on developmental milestones such as the birth defects resulting in her cerebral palsy, childhood fears, phenomenal academic progress in special education programs, and her present limitations, needs and aspirations. "Now, what about music?" Sophie explains how much she has always wanted to be able to make music. The music therapist navigates through her instrument-laden office, pointing out the oversized capos and picks which modify a guitar and autoharp for instant musical accompaniment. "Let's test your dexterity and breath control to determine the most appropriate instruments for more intensive training. Try this autoharp." Sophie is excited about the beautiful chords she is able to strum. She has fun accompanying as the music therapist sings a popular song. To learn more about Sophie's musical taste and experience, the therapist uses a "Music Survey Outline" she has devised to outline her questions (see Figure 4.2).

Sophie and her therapist are ready to discuss their expectations of one another during the course of therapy. It is important to the therapist that Sophie understands the limitations of therapy e.g., that the therapist cannot guarantee Sophie's winning friends simply because she can accompany her peers' singing. Does Sophie agree that she is here not merely to learn music, but also to learn about herself and ways of communicating with others? Is she willing to attempt "homework" assignments beyond music practice, which could involve contacting or attending music groups in the community?

Music Listening
1. Preferred musical style
   Popular: rock, folk, jazz, fusion, blues, Country-Western, soul, easy listening, film scores, other.
   Serious: Renaissance, Baroque, Classical, Romantic, Contemporary, other.
2. Preferred artists
3. Preferred recordings or selections
4. Preferred media
   Instrumental (strings, brass, wind, percussion), vocal, electronic, ensemble, other.
5. Access to music listening
   Via radio, record/cassette player, live performance, concert attendance, community group affiliation, other.
6. Function of music listening to:
   Relax; change feelings; energize; accompany meals, work, exercise, other activities; entertain.

Music Activities (Past or Present Participation)
1. Listening
2. Composing
3. Humming, whistling, tapping feet or clapping
4. Learning about music
4. Talking about music
6. Dancing/ moving to music
7. Singing/playing instruments
8. Participating in community music organizations
9. Taking music classes

Figure 4.2. Music survey outline.

The session ends with the signing of a contract which presents the responsibilities of both parties as well as more practical considerations including the scheduling of sessions, fee, time, mode of payments, length of treatment, and policies concerning confidentiality.

Aims of a First Session

The preceding examples may appear to have little in common because the circumstances surrounding the meetings are unique to each person and therapist. Yet, in each of these sessions, the music therapist is a conscientious observer of behavior, taking mental (if not written) notes of client responses to the setting, the therapist, the music or other presented stimuli, and the individuals in the room. Despite obvious differences in emphasis, the objectives of the three therapists for what is to be accomplished in the first session are the same:

1. to develop rapport,
2. to gather information,
3. to observe,
4. to further define the problem
   and goal, and
5. to outline responsibilities of client
   and therapist.

One of the factors determining how the music therapist will prioritize these aims is the degree of familiarity with the client. Therapists who are part of a clinical team may have discussed the person's background previously with staff or family, in addition to having read extensive files on programming and progress. The person already may have been observed in the clinical, educational, or home setting. Conversely, the itinerant music therapist or one in private practice may know relatively little about the case prior to the first meeting.

In any event, the music therapist will require certain information before meeting the client. Are other professionals or social agencies involved? Is there a parent, guardian, or conservator responsible for the client (who, as with Erica, may be invited to the first session)? What is the reason for referral? Has the client been involved in other programs? If so, what were the objectives and outcomes? Medical and therapeutic history, available through sources other than the person, may offer pertinent data on which to build a viable therapeutic plan. Having gathered such relevant data, the knowledgeable, organized and prepared music therapist should be able to carry out the objectives set for the first encounter.

Developing Rapport

One of the most significant ingredients in any successful therapeutic program is the establishment of a caring relationship between therapist and client. Without it, the most effective techniques may be utterly useless (Brammer, 1973). In creating an atmosphere of trust required for a close working relationship, music therapists may have a distinct advantage. Their primary medium has been termed a means of "instant *rapport*" (Michel, 1979), as it unites people in a common experience. For Erica, whose major difficulty is her inability to enter into any relationship with others, music appears to function as just such a unifying influence. It not only attracts her attention and holds her interest, but also enables the therapist and parents to come physically closer to her and partake in her activity. The musical imitation technique is designed to initiate a nonverbal form of communication, perhaps, an approximation of positive interpersonal interaction. Erica's therapist is encouraged by the changes in his new client's behavior that are already observable.

The music therapist at the mental health center wishes to generate rapport between John and himself as well as other group members. Once again, the nonthreatening nature of group musical experiences brings the group together as they join hands and sing. Opportunities for nonverbal expression and sharing of feelings elicit words of empathy and encouragement, engendering closeness. Establishing trust is a primary goal.

This aspect of musical involvement as a shared experience at a basic emotional level clearly has potential for developing rapport. There is more to the technique, however, than cueing up a CD or demonstrating an autoharp. Sensitive therapists must be able to communicate their genuineness, openness, and warmth. A nonjudgmental posture is at the foundation; tools of active listening build further supports. Conveying acceptance verbally and nonverbally, clarifying messages, and insightful probing are some of the elements which contribute to an effective helping relationship (Loughary & Ripley, 1979). The skillful therapist who demonstrates honest concern may find that musical experiences are capable of enhancing and solidifying the therapeutic alliance.

Sophie's effervescent personality facilitates an almost immediate rapport with the therapist, enabling them to move on with the business of assessment. Regardless of the client's personal character, the music therapist should heed certain recommendations in this early stage of therapy. The following is a list of general suggestions for the therapist who is about to meet a client. Although all of these guidelines may not be applicable to a given clinical situation, the therapist must use personal discretion to determine the relevance of each to the case at hand.

Guidelines for Developing Rapport

1. Introduce yourself and attempt to set your clients at ease by finding out something about them and informing them about yourself, music therapy, and your understanding of why they are there.

2. Remain nonjudgmental during the session, actively observing and listening.

3. Use body language which conveys interest, positive regard, and concern.

4. Ask questions in order to clarify what the person is trying to communicate.

5. Focus on feelings and behavior more than the content of conversation, while reflecting what you see and hear, when appropriate. Save interpretations for later in therapy.

6. Offer opportunities for the person to choose and engage in preferred musical activities. Then, follow up with responses which convey acceptance.

7. Maximize availability of interactive musical activities which emphasize shared experience.

8. Exercise patience. Attempt to learn as much as possible from this first encounter rather than start to solve problems.

Gaining Information

Another objective for the initial therapy session is to gain information which is relevant to the problem at hand and could influence music therapy planning. The music therapist is interested in collecting data in two major areas: 1) the present, and in varying degrees, the past state of the person and problem, and 2) present and past music behavior and responsiveness to music. This is the initial stage of the assessment process articulated more fully in Chapter V.

In the first category, much background material should be obtained from facility records and professional team members prior to meeting the client. In an interview, the person or responsible family members are able to present their perspectives on the presenting problem, the reason for referral, their analysis of the present situation, and expectations of music therapy. To gain a thorough understanding, whenever feasible, the therapist involves the family and others significant to the person or problem in this interview. Their presence will allow the therapist to observe the client within a realistic social context and to identify potential change agents who are accessible to the client outside of music therapy sessions.

While it is not always practical to have the person's social group meet together, the therapist should strive to gain as much information as is available about the home or school environment. Ideally, the music therapist would hold sessions in the setting where the presenting problem is most evident. This not only illuminates the circumstances surrounding the problem, but also ensures a higher probability that the effects observed later in music therapy will generalize to the person's more customary environment. Of course, in a field such as music therapy, access to music materials and an acoustically sound space is also an important criterion for treatment location. Given the practical realities of service delivery, the therapist may not have the option of selecting a treatment site or calling upon others in the person's coterie. In other cases, a therapist focusing on personality reconstruction or other analytically oriented aims might find their individually oriented therapy most desirable in an office removed from the atmosphere encountered daily. These factors must be weighed with consideration of the possible limitations of therapeutic effectiveness when unknown environmental and social variables are influencing the person or contributing to the problem.

In short, the interview should reveal information about the person, relevant history, presenting problem and potential solutions. In this way, Erica's therapist learned the parents' view of her problem and how they coped with it. Sophie's therapist was less interested in background than with her expectations of the future. Information was gathered here through direct questions and answers. In John's first session, the communication was somewhat less direct. Group process created a social context within which perceptions about John and the reason for therapy were expressed. Still more indirect was the musical interactive scheme devised by Erica's therapist to ask the question, "What music do you like?"

The Most Effective Music

This leads to the next area of interest to the music therapist: identifying the person's musical background. The concepts to be tested are responsiveness to music, musical preferences, and abilities. Simple questions may be asked of individuals who are capable of answering. Sophie's therapist has developed a tool specifically for the purpose of determining musical history and preference. But, there are other methods of gathering these data. John is exposed to various musical activities in the group. Music therapy excites nonmusical responses which not only demonstrate musical interest but simultaneously reveal information about the person.

Erica also has access to a variety of musical experiences. As the therapist watches for indicators of enjoyment, e.g., smiling, eye contact with musical stimuli, and active participation, he is discovering potentially reinforcing musical events. In a systematic manner, Erica's therapist times her contact with each set of musical stimuli. The more time spent, the more probable the *reinforcement value* of the activity (Premack, 1959).

Introducing different types of music experiences and determining their relative value on the basis of time spent also has distinct advantages over direct questioning because:

1. individuals incapable of higher cognitive functioning can demonstrate their preferences in this way;

2. people unfamiliar with a wide variety of musical styles or instruments can make clear choices to listen to a particular type of music or participate in a specific activity whereas they may not verbalize a preference at all; and

3. people demonstrate their responsiveness to music when interacting with it, thus offering more information to the therapist. Further, what people actually do is often inconsistent with what they say they do. For these reasons, the procedures may be a more valid measure of preference. Erica's therapist benefits from a first-hand look at music and Erica. With other people, the therapist will allow them to try out and experiment with the different musical sources first, and then, examine their decisions when free to choose between the musical options.

In determining music preferences, the following guidelines are offered:

1. Consider developing a complete performance repertory and recorded inventory of musical styles for interviewing purposes.

2. Present the client with different musical stimuli (circles of musical instruments or recordings) and demonstrate their use, where feasible.
   a. Offer opportunities to participate in activities of choice.
   b. Observe responsiveness vs. lack of interest while involved in each experience.

3. Employ tests of musical abilities as appropriate.

Observing

Careful observation is one of the therapist's most valuable tools. During initial sessions, it informs the therapist about the person's present behavior in an objective way as contrasted with the subjective verbal report of the person. Observing affective behavior enables the therapist to gain greater insight into the feelings behind actions and whether these two elements are compatibly displayed. In this first session, these observations set the stage for more formal assessment.

The music therapy setting is used as a *metaphor* (Haley, 1976) for social, emotional, or educational experiences outside of therapy. That is, the assumption is made that how people behave within the music therapy session is indicative of how they act elsewhere. Problem-solving, dealing with numerous social situations, and interactive patterns are all observable and shapeable in the therapeutic setting. Given the metaphor tenet between therapy and reality, change in therapy should yield change in other areas of one's life. Although transfer of behavioral changes to other situations cannot always be assumed to take place, it is, nevertheless, possible to observe, assess and modify a tremendous variety of skills and social behaviors within the music therapy session.

What to Observe

Music therapy includes a wide variety of activities which call for passive and active responses, physical manipulation, social interaction, emotional reactions, and cognitive skills. Through various music experiences, such as leading a song, a listening task, instrument-playing, and movements to music, the therapist observes specific client responses in such categories as:

1. degree of participation,
2. enjoyment,
3. instruction-following,
4. attention to the task,
5. attention to the therapist,
6. social interaction,
7. fine and gross motor coordination,
8. speech, language skills,
9. appropriate and inappropriate social behavior,
10. affective (emotional) behavior, and
11. musical behavior.

This cursory assessment may fulfill the primary goal of any assessment process identifying outstanding abilities as well as deficits. The therapist will be particularly interested in noting behaviors such as disruptive social actions, which may interfere with learning new skills or participating in a group. Basic skills which are prerequisite to more advanced functioning, such as the ability to pay attention, follow simple instructions and sit in a chair for the duration of one activity, will also be exposed through musical involvement. Simple forms which outline various behaviors and musical activities may be used to record these responses (see Figure 4.3). This preliminary examination is feasible even with a large group of clients when the therapist uses a shorthand method of recording. For instance, rather than commenting on each class of behaviors at the end of an activity, the therapist could chart them entering a "+" for acceptable responses, a "-" for weak or inappropriate responses, and a "0" for questionable responses requiring further observation. This information is not only useful to guide future assessment efforts, but may also assist the music therapist who wishes to group people on the basis of their skills or functioning levels.

Observation plays an important role from the very beginning of music therapy. Whether performed within a carefully contrived structure by a therapist like Erica's or more informally as in John's case, astute observation is an essential component of a therapy program. Therapists who, through careful observation, scrutinize the strengths and weaknesses of those they hope to help should, like a detective, be able to solve some of the personal mysteries which bring them to seek music therapy.

Outlining Responsibilities

Before the person leaves the first session, it is important that certain ground rules or policies be established. A *contract* is a viable means of setting down expectations that therapist and client have of one another. The conditions specified in the contract should be consistent with those of the associated agency or facility as well as with the therapist's and person's own values. People incapable of participation in the process of contracting may have an advocate negotiate on their behalf.

Behavior	Clients (or Activities)						Comments
	1.	2.	3.	4.	5.	6.	
Participation							
Enjoyment							
Appropriate Behavior							
Inappropriate Behavior							
Following Instructions							
Attention to Therapist							
Attention to Task							
Client Interaction							
Fine Motor Coordination							
Gross Motor Coordination							
Speech, Language							
Other							

Client _____
Therapist _____
Description of group _____

Date _____
Observation Period ____ : ____ TO ____ : ____
Observer _____

Figure 4.3. Sample group observation form.

Sophie and her therapist discuss considerations which are important to each of them before signing a statement of mutual agreement. Therapists who fail to identify their responsibilities to clients and possible limitations of therapy may, and perhaps, should be liable for lack of therapeutic success, however that may be defined. On the other hand, a written clarification of some of the conditions of therapy may resolve concerns before they appear. Although each therapist will have to determine the advisability of specificity in the early stages of therapy, the following are options for potential inclusion in the contract:

1. Procedural details: time and length of session, policies and make-up sessions, fees and method of payment, etc.

2. Ethical considerations: ensuring confidentiality, procedures in case of "emergency."

3. Agreement regarding goals of therapy.

4. Agreement regarding therapeutic methods to be employed.

5. Possible limitations of therapy.

6. Explanation of therapist's role and responsibilities which may include holding or attending meetings on the client's status and progress.

7. Statement of the client's voluntary involvement in music therapy and other responsibilities while participating in therapy.

8. Description of evaluation strategies for therapeutic success and conditions of termination.

9. Permission to release photographs, videotapes or other media for special purposes.

In all likelihood, the music therapist will want to stipulate some general policies in the contract at the start of therapy, postponing methodological details until later. The first session should end with therapist and client on their way to developing a working relationship and an understanding of the conditions they will face as music therapy progresses.

Summary

Erica's first music therapy encounter is a productive one. After interviewing her parents, the music therapist is able to make an objective analysis of her musical interest by recording the amount of time she spends interacting with various musical stimuli. After giving her this opportunity to choose musical instruments and recorded music, the therapist gradually introduces himself and the family to the circle of music. A rapport building technique, whereby people are ever so gradually added to Erica's interaction with an instrument, is shown to be effective.

The primary objective of John's first session at the mental health center is to generate a nonthreatening environment in which the opportunity for trust and rapport building is maximized. Active listening and counseling techniques combined with the nonverbal expressive aspects of music accelerate this process.

Sophie's therapist chooses a music survey to determine the best therapeutic musical modality. An interview is the most appropriate way to gather information. This initial session ends with the signing of a contract to delineate responsibilities and expectations of client and therapist.

This chapter also offers guidelines for developing rapport, gaining information, observing, and contracting.

Key Words

Contract
> A mutually agreed upon set of expectations, rules, and policies, governing the behavior of both therapist and client.

Metaphor
> An experience or setting within which behavior is representative or indicative of other life experiences or environments.

Rapport
Closeness or trust which is considered conducive to a warm, understanding and caring environment.
Reinforcement value
The degree to which an activity or material is likely to serve as reinforcement for the behavior, i.e., to result in an increase in the behavior it follows.

References

Brammer, L. M. (1973). *The helping relationship: Process and skills.* Englewood Cliffs, NJ: Prentice-Hall.

Haley, J. (1976). *Problem solving therapy: New strategies for effective family therapy.* New York: Harper & Row.

Loughary, J. W., & Ripley, T. M. (1979). *Helping others help themselves: A guide to counseling skills.* New York: McGraw-Hill.

Michel, D. E. (1979). *Music therapy: An introduction to therapy and special education through music.* Springfield, IL: Charles C. Thomas.

Premack, D. (1959). Toward empirical behavior laws. *Psychological Review, 66,* 286–295.

For Further Reading

Dass, R., & Gorman, P. (1997). *How can I help?* New York: Alfred A. Knopf.

Mahrer, A. R. (1986). *Therapeutic experiencing: The process of change.* New York: W.W. Norton & Company.

Rambo, A. H., Heath, A., & Chenail, R. J. (1993). *Practicing therapy.* New York: W.W. Norton & Company.

Zaro, J. S., Barach, R., Nedelman, D. J., & Dreiblatt, A. S. (1987). *A guide for beginning psychotherapists.* Cambridge: Cambridge University Press.

Do you know that our soul is composed of harmony?
        —Leonardo da Vinci (1452–1519)

Chapter 5

Assessment

Last year, I attended a concert with a friend. We had gone to hear our local symphony orchestra and had not checked the program in advance. I had experienced a particularly challenging week, and was looking forward to an evening of leisure and distraction. When I opened the program booklet, I learned that the orchestra and soloist would be performing Prokofieff's second piano concerto, a piece I had loved, but would not find enjoyable that night. I had listened to this piece while in labor prior to the birth of my still-born daughter, knowing that there was no fetal heartbeat. I had breathed in synchrony with these driving rhythms, swift phrases, and enharmonic tonalities which mirrored my emotions. My associations with this music were vivid and they transported me back to a day of pain and despair.

I realized that earlier in the week, I had led one of my stress reduction sessions in which I had played music without asking group members whether any of this music held particular meaning for them. I had not taken the time to assess their experience or past associations with this music. It struck me that as a music therapist, I, of all people, knew the power that music holds. Failing to assess its potential impact before innocently playing it could have yielded a similarly devastating memory for anyone in the group. It was not my intention for the group to experience anything but physical relaxation at this time, and fortunately, no such negative association was triggered, to my knowledge.

My lesson was clear. I was not to take the music for granted again. I was not to lead a session without performing assessment first.

Assessment is a systematic approach to determining a person's strengths and weaknesses. It involves systematic observation under a special set of circumstances. Observational strategies may be devised to test the quantity and quality of target behaviors as well as related skills and competencies. This chapter covers a general assessment of functioning, music therapy assessment, initial assessment, comprehensive assessment, and ongoing assessment.

A General Assessment of Functioning

Would a music therapist begin therapy by presenting a violin to an aggressive preschooler, a toy piano to an older adult, or a complicated contrapuntal piece for a musically unsophisticated adolescent to perform? Unless there is a special evaluative purpose for these practices, the choice of these activities would be quite absurd. It is obvious that the selected activities are not matched with the clients' present functioning levels or ages.

There are several criteria to consider before starting to plan a music therapy program. Assessment of communication skills will help determine the appropriate vocabulary to be used in music therapy. Cognitive skills will reveal ways in which the client can be expected to learn. Physical abilities, particularly *sensory-motor* or *perceptual-motor* development, must be assessed to determine whether the client is able to meet the perceptual and physical prerequisites of therapeutic activities. An analysis of musical abilities will allow the therapist to offer activities which are appropriate and success-oriented while remaining somewhat challenging. Observations of psycho-social and emotional behavior will afford the therapist the chance to predict how the person will respond to therapeutic experiences. Awareness, self-help, adjustment, vocational needs, and spiritual perspective may be relevant to planning as well.

The music therapist is particularly interested in responses which:

1. are relevant to the goal and target behavior;
2. support other functional skills; and
3. affect how the person will respond in music therapy.

The established goal for therapy will guide the process, and should be the most significant area for assessment. The target behavior is the set of responses toward which therapy will direct its efforts. It identifies an observable behavior to be changed over the course of therapy. Of course, there are other areas which affect the functional capacity of the individual and impinge on the target behavior. How the person communicates, thinks, pays attention, responds, moves, feels, perceives, imagines, acts and interacts are interrelated and important to assess. There are other dimensions of experience which help predict how the person will respond to music and music therapy experiences. An assessment of music preferences and musical abilities is relevant to this process.

The *assessment tool* may be a test, survey or device used to measure the abilities of a person in an identified area. A myriad of assessment devices are available, many of which are standardized, thus giving normative data for comparison with an individual client's performance (Aiken, 1971). For the music therapist's purpose, some tests can be adapted to the musical context; others may be developed for a particular client.

A discriminating assessment tool will:

1. identify strengths and weaknesses;
2. give corroborating evidence of the suitability of the selected goal;
3. help determine target behaviors and specific objectives to guide therapy;
4. disclose other potential goals;
5. detect information about the nature of the target behavior and prerequisite skills; and
6. pinpoint those tasks which the person can and cannot do.

A Music Therapy Assessment

Many professionals question the need for assessment specific to the music therapy setting. Is it not sufficient for the therapist to read a comprehensive report by an independent professional? If the music therapist expects to see change within the walls of the session as well as outside them, then an indication of the client's behavior in the presence of the music therapist and in the music therapy environment is indicated. There are other advantages to a unique music therapy assessment (Michel, 1982). Besides offering opportunities for responses to a variety of stimuli, the music therapy setting is particularly conducive to nonthreatening and anxiety-reducing testing. Individuals who are engaged in enjoyable activities appear relatively free of common testing pressures. In fact, they may be hardly aware that the situation is designed for observation and evaluation.

Another point is that there are certain skills which may be evaluated best within a musical context. Auditory perception and memory, for instance, are two areas with which music is naturally associated. By merely singing a song, individuals reveal their acuity in auditory sequencing, attending, sound blending, and auditory sensitivity. *Auditory discrimination* is tested via a task where listeners describe sound characteristics, e.g., timbre (quality of sound, such as train, car horn, piano), directionality (from where the sound emanates), intensity (loud-soft), pitch (high-low), tempo (fast-slow), and duration (long-short). Then, they are asked to imitate these sounds vocally or on an instrument. The auditory-motor match is analyzed by the degree to which movement to music is correctly imitated or rhythmically coordinated. For even the most profoundly challenged individual, the degree of awareness may be determined by watching for subtle movements to music, e.g., visual tracking or startle responses to loud sounds. At a more sophisticated level, perceptual difficulties are assessed by observing imitation of gross and fine motor movements and locomotor patterns, e.g., skipping, clapping, turning, sliding, running, jumping and hopping.

In a different spectrum, social and emotional reactions to music may be examined using music listening as a projective technique. Verbal and nonverbal responses to a piece of music may be carefully observed, and compatibility between verbal content and affective behavior noted. For instance, does the individual smile while stating that the music brings on sadness? Does the person consistently note somber tones in a generally lilting song? Observations of such responses may provide diagnostic information when care is taken to ensure that conclusions are not drawn hastily. It is tempting to assume that a person with an unusual or unpopular emotional reaction to music may be projecting personality characteristics, when it is equally plausible that strong psychological associations with a particular music selection account for this behavior. In the case of a woman who was informed of her husband's death while she was listening to music, hearing pieces of a similar genre brings about an expected emotional outpouring of great magnitude. In this example, it is easy to make an erroneous interpretation.

The imagery revealed through music listening is another response of interest to music therapists. Musically evoked images offer data to an analytically oriented therapist concerning the perceptual system of the listener (Bonny & Savary, 1983). The individual's imagery is said to project feelings, motivation, outlook on life, and significant personal events which are less accessible cognitively (Sheikh, 1983).

The purpose of such musical projective techniques proposed in this data-based model is not to examine personality traits or inner states as much as it is to provide opportunities to observe a wealth of social and emotional behaviors in a carefully controlled context. As emotional changes become evident through observations of language, motor and visceral behaviors, the therapist further articulates a goal which identifies target behaviors as opposed to diagnostic classifications (Cone & Hawkins, 1983). The observation process provides more direct evidence than would be obtained by asking clients how they would respond to a given situation, and further, it analyzes nonverbal behavior which is also significant to the person's experience.

In still another setting, when members of a clinical treatment team consider music therapy as a related service, they have the opportunity to refer a child for music therapy assessment. When that assessment demonstrates that music therapy is necessary for the child to benefit from special education, music therapy may be written into the child's Individualized Education Plan (IEP). An increasing number of music therapists are being requested to perform these assessments which play a critical role in determining whether a school district will provide this related service.

There are three primary indications for assessment:

1. Initial Assessment. Assessment is performed at the beginning of the therapeutic process to guide music therapy and establish a point at which to begin. This process is always indicated, and generally focuses on the treatment goal.

2. Comprehensive Assessment. An individual may be referred for music therapy assessment only. This is usually a more comprehensive effort to determine the feasibility of music therapy services and examine many aspects of functioning. It may also be advisable when the individual has difficulty complying with other forms of standardized assessment. This is particularly the case with children who have very short attention spans, individuals who are greatly distressed, and cognitively impaired older adults. Music therapy offers a less threatening environment where individuals may benefit from the structured and nonthreatening setting.

3. Ongoing Assessment. Assessment is used in an ongoing manner to evaluate music therapy. Assessment tools may be administered repeatedly throughout the course of therapy, usually pre-, mid- and post-treatment. Systematic observation is another useful way to examine behaviors over time. The nature of the target behaviors will determine whether a specific assessment tool or observation technique is most suitable.

Initial Assessment

The extent to which assessment strategies are implemented depends upon the goal of therapy and the therapist's orientation. Music therapists seek as complete a picture of the total person as is feasible, given their role within a clinical team. Assessment procedures may be as simple as asking a client to partake in a variety of music activities or as structured as administering a standardized test. Before beginning formal assessment, the music therapist might consider the following criteria:

1. Which of the following skills could have greatest impact on the target behavior and music therapy plan?
   a. communication—verbal and nonverbal expression, receptive and expressive language
   b. cognitive—thinking, processing, learning style
   c. physical—general physical health and status; *sensory-motor* or *perceptual-motor* skills, including hearing, seeing, perceiving, touching, smelling, moving
   d. musical—interest, responsiveness, preference, vocal and instrumental abilities, pitch discrimination, rhythmic perception, creativity
   e. psycho-social—attention, self-awareness, self-concept, self-esteem, participation, cooperation, compliance, relationship to therapist, interpersonal skills, and interaction with others
   f. emotional—affect and feeling
   g. other relevant areas—including psychological or educational needs, activities of daily living, personal adjustment, leisure, vocational and spiritual needs, etc.

2. What evaluative information already exists?
   a. from other professionals
   b. from the first session

3. How can each of these skills be measured most efficiently?
   a. through observation of behaviors
   b. with an existing assessment device designed to test skill levels
   c. with an original assessment tool

4. What music experiences provide observation opportunities or analogues for the type of skills requiring assessment?

5. What other conditions or settings will be used for assessment purposes?

    a. How will each skill be measured?

    b. Where and within what context will it be examined?

A Clinical Example: Ralph

Consider Ralph, a 23-year-old man, who was blinded in an automobile accident. Still recuperating at home from numerous contusions, he is increasingly more morose and despondent each day, refusing to care for himself or attempt any of the activities which he enjoyed prior to this traumatic event. Referred by his social worker, the music therapist visits Ralph at home. At the completion of their first session, the therapist enters the following narrative account:

1. a. Communication—Ralph is articulate when speaking with family members. He does not volunteer information to the music therapist, and is reluctant to speak.

    b. Cognitive—Ralph is a highly intelligent, high school-educated man.

    c. Physical—Ralph's only outstanding impairment is blindness. He is extremely well-coordinated. His mobility has been greatly enhanced with a guide dog. There is no history of any previous perceptual problem.

    d. Musical—Musical interests are extensive. He is trained in jazz piano and owns a piano, but has not played in several years. Having performed a few times in local coffee houses, he was interested in resuming piano lessons before the accident, but sees his potential as extremely limited now.

    e. Psycho-social—He shuns visitors and has asked his mother (with whom he lives) to tell his friends that he is dead. He reluctantly interacts with the therapist, using monosyllables to respond, if he answers at all.

f. Emotional—His depressive state since the accident is the greatest problem to overcome. He has little appetite and no motivation to dress or leave his bedroom.

2. a. Social Worker's Evaluation—Ralph was referred to music therapy because of the extreme emotional response to his disability. When he mentioned to his social worker that giving up his musical hobby was very difficult, she immediately phoned the music therapist. The social worker and physician remain valuable sources of background information on this case.

   b. Initial Music Therapy Evaluation—Ralph stated that he always enjoyed improvising at the keyboard. Since he rarely used sheet music, he insisted that he must watch the keys intently in order to play well. He presently believes that his playing will never be the same. When asked to attempt some familiar pieces at the piano, he was reticent. Then, after one short measure using his right hand, he turned away and began to cry. Ralph appears physically capable, but not psychologically ready to return to piano study. A cursory examination leads the therapist to articulate the following goals: To resume regular social activities and increase positive social interaction. In the short-term, the immediate goal is to partake of leisure activities and interact with others on a regular basis. This leads to the following target behaviors:

      Participation in activities outside his
      own room, specifically piano practice
      Talking with others.

3. Ralph will chart the time spent out of his bedroom, at the piano, and talking with others daily.

4. Success-oriented piano lessons and informal counseling will serve as the primary treatment modalities. When he develops

self-confidence and ventures beyond his room more often, Ralph will be encouraged to invite friends to hear him play and to participate in community musical events.

5. Until Ralph begins to leave the house regularly, assessment of progress will be performed during music therapy sessions. Ralph will also be self-monitoring through the use of charts at other times during the week.

Comprehensive Assessment

A more comprehensive assessment is called for when a person is not yet referred for music therapy, and there is a question regarding whether the person will be able to benefit from music therapy. This type of initial assessment may be particularly useful to the music therapist who is called upon as a team member to assist in the person's overall diagnostic or assessment process. The Assessment Report may follow a similar outline as the Initial Assessment, but goes into greater depth. Background information and recommendations are also integrated into the report. The following is a more comprehensive assessment report on a child with pervasive developmental disability who is referred by an IEP team.

A Clinical Example: Laura D.

I. Background

Laura D. attends a first grade inclusion class. Her diagnosis is pervasive developmental disorder—autism, and she is seven years old. The IEP team has referred Laura for a music therapy assessment because she is not participating in the classroom, and they are questioning whether she is learning anything in this setting. She displays little spontaneous language and a flat affect. Laura's parents would like to have her remain in the inclusion classroom, which is the least restrictive environment. They are hopeful that music therapy could potentially help her integrate into the larger classroom.

Laura's father, Mr. D., reports that Laura memorizes the words to songs when she watches television and videotapes. She has a large repertoire of songs, including "The Eency Weency Spider,"

"Twinkle, Twinkle Little Star," "Rudolf the Red Nosed Reindeer," and many Christmas Carols. Her reaction to music is unique in that she is interested and successful at these tasks as opposed to other academic tasks. She is attentive for long periods of time when engaged in singing and musical activities. Laura plays independently when involved with musical instruments. This response is unique to music as she shows little interest in other activities. She is highly involved and happy when engaged with music.

II. Initial Observations

At the Assessment Session, Laura went immediately to the drum set. She engaged quickly in beating the drum. Her eye contact and attention remained firmly focused on her playing.

According to her father, when she enters a novel setting with a stranger, Laura is fearful and reactive. She maintained a calm affect and showed immense contentment among the musical instruments. She answered the therapist's questions comfortably. According to her father, these are all highly unusual responses for Laura. The musical interactions seemed to set the stage for an easy rapport. When asked, she cooperated in playing new instruments which were introduced into the session.

III. Observed Responses To Music Therapy
Communication

Laura answered the therapist's simple questions about her music preference by using single words or phrases. She demonstrated good receptive language by picking up the correct musical instruments on the therapist's request with only one error. Her vocabulary is extremely limited, but she recognized all of the musical instruments in the room.

Although Laura does not often express herself verbally, she initiated her desire to open the guitar case by saying very clearly, "I want to play guitar." This was much to her father's surprise. He commented that she rarely self-initiates a conversation nor is she able to so freely express her wishes. Furthermore, she does not communicate in full sentences. Her vocabulary has increased around her song repertoire. She knew that a guitar was hidden in a case of that shape. During the Christmas holidays, Laura learned many new songs and enjoyed singing them often.

Drum-beating generated multiple spontaneous behaviors, including singing. She sang 90% of the words to two children's songs, "Jingle Bells," and "Mary Had a Little Lamb." Singing was very natural for her, and she sang with far greater fluency and volume than she spoke.

Cognition

Laura complied moderately with verbal instructions regarding how to play different instruments. When she was presented with a variety of musical instruments, physical guidance was necessary to teach her how to play a new percussion instrument. Such an approach was successful in teaching her new skills.

Physical Ability

Laura is in generally good health and she is physically able. She did not track instruments visually because her attention was so highly focused on playing. She demonstrated reasonable fine motor coordination by grasping mallets appropriately, but displayed difficulty in hitting single notes of the soprano xylophone.

Music Preferences and Abilities

Laura alternated from drum to cymbals and back to the drum without difficulty. She enjoyed exploring new instruments and made up songs which she sang along with great pleasure. She followed simple rhythms on percussion.

On the piano, Laura was able to follow a three-note pattern. She improvised easily on the black keys. In this brief assessment session, she demonstrated that she was capable of learning new musical patterns.

Psycho-social and Emotional Skills

Laura had a clear preference to play independently as opposed to interacting with the therapist. She initiated participation on every instrument given to her, including piano, drum, cymbal, autoharp, and other simple percussion. She was resistant to sharing the instrument with the therapist, preferring to sing the songs she knew and to continue playing on her instrument of choice.

When the therapist began a musical mirroring exercise to engage her in following various rhythms, Laura correctly repeated simple rhythms. She preferred to lead the rhythmic patterns as opposed to following. She displayed an assertiveness and confidence while drumming many complex rhythms.

Over the hour, she began to engage in cooperative improvisation on xylophones and drums. She became more responsive to the therapist by the end of the hour, looking up and smiling several times during their final improvisation.

IV. Overall Observations

Laura remained attentive to the tasks for approximately one hour without any detachment from the various musical activities. Her interest in music is exceptional. Music activities held her attention for long periods of time when she appeared riveted to the musical tasks. In the short assessment session, she was able to demonstrate new learning on the keyboard, an indication that piano instruction may be used to introduce and reinforce new concepts and skills. Although her spontaneous language is limited, her spontaneous singing is widespread.

V. Recommendations

Music is remarkably reinforcing for Laura. Her behavior reflects a capacity to learn a variety of skills through involvement in specific music-related activities. Music therapy is indicated for children like Laura who respond so actively and positively to music. Her language acquisition may be strengthened through singing new songs and associating the written and sung words. Her motor organization and coordination may be enhanced through playing instruments, and academic skills may be developed by learning the musical competencies that she is so motivated to gain. Involvement in weekly music therapy sessions would offer Laura an opportunity to develop rapport with a therapist and potentially, other children in the classroom. It is recommended that the music therapist work with the entire class on a limited basis to help integrate Laura into working with her peers.

Ongoing Assessment

When assessment is performed more than once, it becomes part of an ongoing process to evaluate therapy. The therapist uses an assessment tool as a *pretest* offered prior to the onset of therapeutic intervention, a midtest (or series of midtests) which checks progress as therapy continues, and finally, as a *posttest* to determine overall treatment efficacy. In this way, test performance offers a measure of progress toward the goal. Data which are gathered may be displayed in tables or graphs to document change during the course of therapy.

When administering an assessment tool for purposes of pre- and posttesting, it is important that the examiner refrain from delivering any hints, cues or praise for desired responses. Often, in order to maintain appropriate behavior in the test environment, praise for sitting still, attending to the task, answering questions or attempting a response is advisable. However, any therapist intervention relative to test responses themselves may influence the results and should be avoided.

When the particular pretest-posttest is selected as the measure of client change, there are two significant factors to consider. First, the test must measure what it purports to measure. This characteristic, known as *validity*, is often questioned when concepts such as intelligence or musical talent are assessed through various test items. Secondly, repeated testing by the same device should yield similar results. This attribute, test-retest *reliability*, should be scrutinized routinely by offering multiple opportunities for the same responses and comparing results. Variability in responding on two or more administrations of the same test beyond that normally expected in human performance could be interpreted to mean that the test is not a reliable measure of change. In this case, steps should be taken to revise the test, retest with a more reliable device, or account for factors which might be affecting results.

An Original Assessment Tool for Finger Dexterity

Music therapists may use their innate creativity to develop original tools for assessment. The following example attests to the simplicity that may be achieved in a test (see Figure 5.1). It is an original assessment tool for finger dexterity, applied in the music therapy setting. It provided just the sort of information required for determining a treatment strategy for the rehabilitation of a stroke victim. Note the results in Figure 5.1. The client is only able to make an audible sound with the index finger, and then, only sporadically on the piano. In this case, the music therapy program began with learning songs which required the repetitive use of one index finger on the piano.

					FINGERS		
Pretest	Hand	Instrument	Thumb	Index	Middle	Ring	Little
1	Right	Piano	—	+	—	0	0
1	Right	Drum	—	0	—	—	—
1	Left	Piano	0	+	—	0	—
1	Left	Drum	—	0	0	—	0
2	Right	Piano	—	0	—	0	—
2	Right	Drum	—	0	—	—	—
2	Left	Piano	—	+	—	0	—
2	Left	Drum	0	0	—	—	0

KEY: + = moved correct finger and made audible sound
       — = made an attempt, but moved more than one finger, or the
            sound was not audible
       0 = made no attempt

Pretest Results:

Pretest	No. Correct	No. Attempted
1	2	10
2	1	12
Mean Pretest Score	1½	11

Figure 5.1. Original assessment tool for finger dexterity.

An Original Pretest-Posttest Assessment for Socialization and Agitation

The goals for a group of older adults in early to middle stages of dementia was to improve socialization and decrease agitation. Since attendance at the group was variable, the music therapist decided to test the levels of these behaviors in each group member immediately before and after each music therapy session. The therapist devised the rating scale shown in Figure 5.2 for the target behaviors of social interaction and agitation/calmness. The scale defined five levels of behavior: two negative behaviors, one neutral for no observable observation, and two positive behaviors. This information was useful for charting purposes and for determining the efficacy of music therapy procedures.

Participant_____ Date_____
Observer_____

Assess the following:

Level of **social interaction** before music therapy:

-2   -1   0   1   2

Level of **social interaction** immediately after music therapy:

-2   -1   0   1   2

Level of **agitation/calmness** before music therapy:

-2   -1   0   1   2

Level of **agitation/calmness** immediately after music therapy:

-2   -1   0   1   2

Figure 5.2. Music therapy assessment pre- post-session. (*Continued on next page*).

An Original Assessment Tool for Responsiveness to Music

To devise a test for responsiveness to music, the therapist has organized a series of tasks which offer the opportunity to observe this behavior in different contexts. Consider the grid in Figure 5.3. The therapist provides four types of music experiences: singing, movement to music, rhythm activities, and keyboard performance. Within each of these modalities, there are a series of graduated events which take the form of baseline, prompted, independent and collaborative tasks.

KEY FOR RATING OBSERVATIONS

Level of **social interaction**: RATE BEFORE AND AFTER SESSION

Inappropriate interactions include the following:

    a) physical communication - any pushing or hitting, turning or moving away from speaker, physically resisting when asked to join others

    b) verbal communication - any negative words showing resistance, anger or frustration

    c) other nonverbal communication - facial grimaces, closing eyes or looking away from person

Mark -2 for any two of the above behaviors or sentences/phrases

Mark -1 for any one of the above behaviors or sentences/phrases

Mark 0 for no interaction

Appropriate interactions include the following:

    a) physical communication - approaching another person in a comfortable or friendly manner, reaching for a person's hand, moving toward a person in an non-threatening way

    b) verbal communication - any positive words showing interest, friendliness, comfort or happiness

    c) other nonverbal - smiling, eye contact with person

Mark 1 for any one of the above behaviors or sentences/phrases

Mark 2 for any two of the above behaviors or sentences/phrases

Level of **agitation/calmness**: RATE BEFORE AND AFTER SESSION

Agitation is any movement of the body in a nonfunctional or dysfunctional way. (Do not include tremors or movements which are neurologically controlled, thus not under person's control)

Mark -2 for any two or more parts of the body (each arm, hand, leg, foot, torso, head) which display agitation; or movement of whole body

Mark -1 for one part of the body which displays agitation

Mark 0 for no observable display or agitation or calmness

Calmness is observed through absence of rigidity or obvious tension in the body and face, vocalizations (ahh, ohh) or verbalizations indicating relaxation or comfort

Mark 1 if the body displays calmness as described above

Mark 2 for any two or more indications of calmness, any vocalization or verbalization described above

Figure 5.2. (*Continued.*)

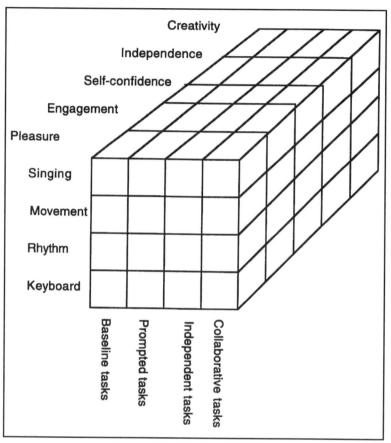

Figure 5.3. Conceptual model for observing responsiveness to music.

Baseline tasks consist of activities which are within the person's competencies. The therapist requests:

Singing	"Sing me a song you know"
Movement	"Move to the music any way you like"
Rhythm	"Clap with me to the music"
Keyboard	"Play any tune on the keyboard"

Prompted tasks place gradually more demands on the person with music of greater complexity. The therapist starts with a task similar to the baseline, then changes the musical stimulus (song, movement, rhythm and melody) to make it more difficult to imitate. The therapist says:

Singing — "Sing this back to me"

Movement — "Follow me" or "Mirror me"

Rhythm — "Watch what I clap (play) and then you clap (play) the same way"

Keyboard — "Play what I play on the keyboard"

Independent tasks provide opportunities to show what the person is capable of doing. The therapist prompts:

Singing — "Make up a song about (a particular interest)"

Movement — "Show me a way to move to this music"

Rhythm — "Clap (play) a rhythm for this music"

Keyboard — "Make up a melody on the keyboard"

Collaborative tasks involve interacting with the music. The therapist improvises, offering some musical suggestions and invites the person to enter the improvisation:

Singing — "Let's make up a song together"

Movement — "Let's move together"

Rhythm — "Let's play together"

Keyboard	"I'll play a melody and you play something along with me"

The person's performance on each task is scored as correct responses, approximations and incorrect responses. In addition, the therapist rates the person on a scale from one to five on each of five dimensions of responsiveness (see Figure 5.4).

Rating

Response	1 strongly negative response	2 negative response	3 no response	4 positive response	5 strongly positive response
Pleasure					
Engagement					
Self-confidence					
Independence					
Creativity					

Figure 5.4. Rating scale for responsiveness to music.

The person's performance is rated most easily when the experiences are videotaped. The ratings of two independent observers can be compared to determine reliability (see Chapter VII for instructions on calculating inter-observer reliability). The results of this assessment demonstrate several ways in which an individual may display responsiveness to music. They also indicate the person's musical strengths and weaknesses.

Summary

Assessment means more than the casual application of a given test to ascertain a score. It provides an initial, comprehensive, or ongoing measurement of communication, cognitive, physical, musical, psycho-social, emotional, and other behaviors. An assessment of functioning is performed to determine strengths and weaknesses in the target behavior, and in other functions which may affect either this behavior or the formulation of a music therapy plan.

Key Words

Assessment
> A systematic approach to the evaluation, appraisal or observation of a person's strengths and weaknesses in preparation for treatment planning.

Assessment tool
> A test, device, form, or instrument which is developed for the purpose of measuring strengths and weaknesses in a given area.

Auditory discrimination
> Distinguishing between sounds or changes in sounds.

Perceptual-motor
> Pertaining to the organization and interpretation of a stimulus and its motor response.

Posttest
> An assessment of skills which is administered following a therapeutic intervention or at the end of a designated experimental phase.

Pretest
> An assessment of skills which is administered prior to a therapeutic intervention or experimental condition.

Reliability (test-retest)
> The degree to which a test or observation is consistent.

Sensory-motor
> Pertaining to the combination or processing of a sensory stimulus and motor response.

Validity
> The degree to which a test measures what it purports to measure.

References

Aiken, L. R., Jr. (1971). *Psychological testing and assessment.* Boston: Allyn & Bacon.

Bonny, H., & Savary, L. M. (1973). *Music and your mind: Listening with a new consciousness.* New York: Harper & Row.

Cone, J. D., & Hawkins, R. P. (Eds.). (1983). *Behavioral assessment: New directions in clinical psychology.* New York: Brunner-Mazel.

Michel, D. E. (1982). Music therapy for handicapped children: Assessment. In B. Lathom, & C. T. Eagle, (Eds.), *Project music monograph series.* Washington, DC: National Association for Music Therapy.

Sheikh, A. A. (1983). *Imagery: Current theory, research, and application.* New York: Wiley.

For Further Reading

Buros, O. K. (1978). *The eighth mental measurements yearbook.* Highland Park, NJ: Gryphon Press.

Cassity, M. D., & Cassity, J. E. (1994). Psychiatric music therapy assessment and treatment in clinical training facilities with adults, adolescents, and children. *Journal of Music Therapy, 31,* 2-30.

Coleman, K. A., & Brunk, B. K. (1999). *Special education music therapy assessment process handbook.* Grapevine, TX: Prelude Music Therapy.

Cronbach, L. J. (1970). *Essentials of psychological testing.* New York: Harper & Row.

Hall, R. V. (1975). *Managing behavior.* Lawrence, KS: H & H Enterprises.

McConaughy, S. H., & Achenbach, T. M. (1996). *Empirically based assessment of child and adolescent psychopathology: Practical applications* (2nd ed.). London: Sage.

Mittler, P. (1970). *The psychological assessment of mental and physical handicaps.* London: Methuen.

Salvia, J., & Ysseldyke, J. E. (1978). *Assessment in special and remedial education*. Boston: Houghton Mifflin.

Wheeler, J. J., & Griggs-Drane, E. R. (1997). The use of functional assessment procedures and individualized schedules in the treatment of autism: Recommendations for music therapists. *Music Therapy Perspectives*, 15, 87–93.

It takes a long time to become young.
—*Pablo Picasso (1881–1973)*

Chapter 6

Goals, Objectives and Target Behaviors

I am a very goal-directed person. That is how I managed to write this textbook. I knew what I wanted to write. I defined what I wanted to include, and wrote an outline. I had a long-term goal, to write a textbook for music therapists, and I set a specific objective, to complete *The New Music Therapist's Handbook*. The outline helped me establish objectives which made the task seem workable and I identified some deadlines to keep me on-task. Completing each section of a chapter by a prescribed date allowed me to see my accomplishments build into an entire book.

In some ways, writing a book is easier than establishing goals and objectives for a music therapy client. The behavior of people is nothing like the pages of a book. Thankfully, people are unique, evolving beings whose actions can never be predicted fully. Our goals and objectives are complicated by the histories we bring to the moment, and the events around us which shape whether or not we can accomplish them.

This chapter attempts to clarify the process of establishing goals and objectives, and offers guidelines for defining target behaviors as a focus for therapy. After performing the initial assessment, the music therapist reviews the goal and target behavior(s), and establishes behavioral objectives to reach this goal. In this chapter, we learn the process through the cases of Joshua, Ann and Michael. As we participate in their music therapist's' decision-making, we learn how the same criteria may be applied to all three distinctly different cases. We follow each therapist's thinking process as problems generate target behaviors and therapeutic goals give rise to objectives. As the therapist learns how to observe target behaviors, their current levels are better understood. The therapist continues to analyze these target behaviors by using different methods of observation and by performing a functional analysis, where feasible. The chapter describes the multifaceted process of clarifying problems and goals, defining target behaviors, and setting behavioral objectives.

Identifying Problems, Behaviors and Goals

Joshua has been institutionalized at a large state residential treatment program for the last 18 of his 20 years. His diagnosis was updated from "profound retardation" to "pervasive developmental disorder" in keeping with changes in special education terminology. The staff is hopeful that he will be able to start a vocational training program at a community-based workshop.

Ann is old and sick. It could be said that this is the problem. After an energetic and successful career as a teacher, she must now rely on others to assist her with the most basic daily living tasks such as toileting and eating. She seems to have given up the struggle to help herself. At the skilled nursing facility, she does not even look at the nurse's aides who help her with basic activities of self care. She stares at the ceiling from her bed during waking hours.

Michael says that he does not have a problem. His third grade teacher disagrees. Michael says the teacher is the problem. He is bored with classroom activities, and prefers to spend his time playing tricks and bothering his classmates. He has been diagnosed with attention deficit/hyperactivity disorder.

Fortunately, Joshua's residence, Ann's nursing home, and Michael's school each have a music therapist on staff. As part of the team of concerned professionals, the music therapist helps decide what to do in each case. The team is confronted with the challenge of identifying the problem or target behavior for therapy.

The Real Problem

At the residence, the team meeting focuses on Joshua's potential for workshop placement. He appears to have the prerequisite skills necessary for admittance. He has made consistent progress in social and perceptual-motor development, has learned some basic academics, and displays no disruptive behavior. The team decides to concentrate therapeutic efforts on those skills necessary for success at the workshop. Joshua has little opportunity to practice fine motor tasks like those required in simple assembly jobs, and sometimes has difficulty manipulating and grasping small objects. It is agreed that, for now, improvement in fine motor coordination is the most important goal.

The nursing staff is caring for Ann's physical needs as best they can. The music therapist is the professional whose primary responsibility is meeting the patient's psychological and social needs. After observing Ann with her family, the therapist decides that the problem may be seen as a lack of behavior. Ann is unresponsive to the environment and non-interactive with others. Records reveal that, though weak, she is capable of speech and movement, but chooses not to engage in these activities. The therapist ponders a realistic goal. Will she ever get out of her bed, care for herself, and happily stride down the hall, chatting with others? Perhaps, it is advisable to consider a more probable short-term objective. At least, she opens her eyes when awake. The first step would seem to have her focus visually on an object or person.

At Michael's school, a group of teachers, parents, and other support personnel are meeting to construct the IEP (Alley, 1979; Levine & Wexler, 1981). Michael's test scores reflect little academic progress in the last year. The teacher advises the staff that Michael is capable of greater achieve-

ment. When his attention is on his lessons, he accomplishes a great deal. Unfortunately, he spends a major part of the school day out of his seat, disrupting his peers' concentration. Michael says he does not like school and cannot stay in his chair in that "stupid classroom." His mother reports that as soon as he comes home, Michael turns on the radio full blast, and proceeds to run about the house, singing along with his favorite rock songs. Given his interest in music, the IEP team refers Michael to a music therapist in an attempt to control disruptive behavior.

These three clinical situations exemplify distinctly different people, settings, and problems. When first introduced, Joshua's, Ann's, and Michael's problems are presented as institutionalization, physical deterioration, and lack of problem recognition, respectively. As we become privy to team discussions, however, we learn that these are not necessarily the real problems. Rather, there are a series of behaviors which are amenable to change, and will form the focus of therapy (Madsen & Madsen, 1998).

Identifying Target Behaviors

In Joshua's case, the behavior of interest is not a "problem" behavior at all. Central to therapeutic intervention at this time is improvement in fine motor coordination. The team comes to this decision after setting a goal (placement in a community-based workshop) and examining the skills required to meet the goal (fine motor coordination). Having met other prerequisites, Joshua must improve finger dexterity to achieve optimal success in the program. Finger dexterity, perhaps more specifically, grasping small objects, is identified as the target behavior for treatment.

Ann does not engage in very much behavior at all. In an attempt to identify an area for change, the therapist looks for an approximation of awareness in Ann. "Staring at the ceiling" is pinpointed as a problem behavior. "Visual focusing on an object or person" is a more desirable and incompatible behavior to replace it. In this case, visual focusing is selected as the target behavior.

Michael, in contrast, exhibits an array of clearly unacceptable behaviors. In his classroom, his behavior disrupts his own concentration and that of others. Overactivity, manifesting itself in inappropriate ways, is the problem which comes to the attention of the IEP team. Disruptive behavior is easily identified as the target problem. But, decreasing a behavior without substituting an appropriate and functional set of responses is an incomplete solution to the problem. Perhaps, the team is already anticipating a way to increase positive social behaviors by referring Michael for music therapy. They acknowledge 1) an inappropriate target behavior to be decreased: out-of-seat behavior, and 2) an appropriate target behavior to increase: attention to a task.

The examples illustrate various decision-making tactics for both setting goals and identifying target behaviors. A target behavior is not necessarily a problem behavior. It is, rather, a set of responses toward which therapy will direct its efforts. In most cases, a client is referred to a clinical facility or to music therapy, in particular, because of a problem. Obviously, the target behavior should relate to the problem and its alleviation, but may involve a constructive set of skills or competing behaviors. Joshua's successful completion of the vocational training program may lead to eventual deinstitutionalization. Ann's efforts to focus on others may help her to deal with her age and illness. Michael's substitution of more socially acceptable behaviors will, undoubtedly, assist him to achieve more in school.

Setting Goals

Goals, indicating expected outcomes in the targeted area, are clarified, based on the reason for referral and the information gleaned from the assessment. They offer a purpose for therapy as well as a direction. Goals may be long-term (Joshua's deinstitutionalization), or short-term (his successful completion of the vocational program), but the terms themselves are relative.

Ann's *long-term goal* may be to initiate positive social interaction with others outside of her room. A more immediate, or *short-term goal* would involve an increased awareness of others. Michael's long-term goal is to improve scholastic achievement and eliminate disruptive activity overall. In the shorter term, the therapist would seek to minimize disruptions in the classroom. Although they may be stated broadly, goals must be amenable to definition, observation, and measurement. After all, one of the reasons for setting these expectations is to facilitate an objective evaluation of changes throughout therapy.

Criteria for Selecting Goals and Target Behaviors

There are numerous criteria to consider when selecting goals and target behaviors:

1. Value: Does this behavior have major impact on present functioning? Could change in this area positively affect other related behaviors? Is this the most important area to change?

2. Prerequisites: Is the goal too far removed from the present behavior? If prerequisite behaviors have not been met, do these constitute more appropriate target behaviors and goals?

3. Interference: Are there inappropriate social behaviors which interfere with achievement of the goal? If so, ought these be targeted for change first?

4. Assessment: Is the target behavior able to be observed and measured over time?

5. Referral: Was the client referred for a specific area of remediation? Does the target behavior reflect the reason for seeking music therapy?

6. Agreement: Do others working with the client agree that this is the most appropriate target area? Secondly, does the client (if capable) agree on this focus for therapy and believe that the goal is attainable?

7. Success: Is there a relatively high probability that this behavior can be changed and the goal can be reached? Does the music therapist have sufficient control over the behavior?

8. Foundation: Is there evidence that this behavior truly requires change? Do data exist to support the view that this is, indeed, a problem?

9. Efficiency: Is there reason to believe that music therapy is the most appropriate treatment? Is it possible for the therapist to devote the necessary time or intensity to attain the goal?

Defining Target Behaviors

Defining the target behavior is essential to objective measurement of change. To facilitate reliable recording, the definition must be extremely precise, presenting clearly observable behaviors. Although it may appear more desirable to define a broad spectrum of behaviors in hopes that therapy will influence a variety of responses, this temptation should be resisted. It must be understood that while a single target behavior is selected, the therapist is not limited to treating this behavior to the exclusion of all others. In fact, while some therapists will deal primarily with changing this behavior, others may view the target as the most important of several problems/behaviors or as a symptom of other difficulties.

One advantage of music therapy is that when one specific behavior is treated, incidental learning of other non-targeted musical and non-musical skills is widespread. Whether the therapist chooses a direct or indirect approach to meeting the client's explicit needs, the target behavior never stands alone. This behavior affects and is affected by a network of behaviors and factors which will influence one another to varying degrees. For the purpose of this music therapy model, the target behavior serves as the principal indicator of change. The outcome of therapy may be evaluated by observing changes in this behavior, regardless of the process used to make those changes.

Because of its central role in the treatment plan, the target behavior should be defined carefully. The details of its parameters should be conceptualized and described so that any two observers of this behavior would agree that it has or has not occurred. Ensuring a high degree of *inter-observer agreement* or reliability is critical in order to present believable results.

A complete behavioral description, or *response definition*, should include the following:

1. A descriptor: a concise descriptive term for the target behavior;
2 Boundaries of the behavior: detailed explanations of where, when, and what responses must occur;
3. Observational information: whether the behavior is discrete (where the number of times a response occurs is recorded) or is continuous (where the length of time it occurs is of greatest interest); and
4. Borderline responses: examples of behaviors which constitute target behaviors and those which are similar, but should not be considered.

Examples

At Joshua's facility, discussion with the occupational therapist, examination of test results, and a brief observation of Joshua reveal that pincer grasp is his most basic problem. The music therapist defines:

Grasping: Picking up a small, thin object (size of a quarter) from a group or box of such objects with the thumb and index finger. The tips of the fingers must be used (any part between the top of the nail and the beginning of the second joint in the finger), and the object must be lifted to eye level and held in place for at least six seconds. If the object shifts its position between the fingers while being held up, even if it is unreleased, this would not represent a correct response. Grasping is recorded as the frequency of correct responses calculated as a percentage of correct responses out of total attempts.

"Visual focusing on an object or person" is described by Ann's music therapist:

> Visual focusing: Having the gaze in both eyes directed toward a specified object or a person's eyes which are located approximately one and one-half feet away. Additionally, when the object or person moves six or more inches, the eyes should shift within two seconds to focus on the new position. Even if the object or person is, at first, directly in front of the eyes, the shift in focus is required to test the response. The eyes need not follow the object or person constantly in its movement, but must locate this new position within two seconds. Focusing is recorded as frequency of appropriate shifts in focus, calculated as a percentage of responses out of total trials. (A trial is defined as a change in position of the stimulus object or eyes by the therapist.)

In Michael's case, there is an inappropriate behavior to be decreased. The teacher suggests that out-of-seat behavior occurs with great frequency and is Michael's major difficulty. This response is defined as it occurs during academic work time in the classroom:

> Out-of-seat behavior: The number of seconds spent away from seat or place designated by the teacher for a given academic activity without permission. Out-of-seat means that no part of the body below the waist is touching the seat. The only exception is in the case of standing on the chair which is considered out-of-seat. Kneeling on a chair or placing one leg on the chair is not considered "out-of-seat;" neither is leaving the seat on the teacher's request. (The teacher must specify where the student is required to be during each recording period and the conditions under which the student may leave his place.) The duration of the behavior is recorded, yielding a percentage of seconds out-of-seat during the total observation time.

The music therapist's positive approach to behavioral change necessitates the description of positive behavior to replace the identified problem. "Attention to the task" is a response which is not only somewhat incompatible with being away from one's seat, but also can be ameliorated in the music therapy setting, and subsequently, transferred to the classroom.

> Attention to the task: The number of seconds spent looking at the teacher or materials specified by her, reading or writing. "Looking at" means visual gaze is focused in the direction of teacher or materials. Attention to the task includes time engaged in any one of the above activities so that writing is considered a positive response even if the student is looking away from materials. (The teacher must specify the materials required for the lesson.) The duration of the behavior yields a percentage of seconds attending to the task during the total observation period.

Setting Objectives

In the same way that the response definition behaviorally specifies the problem or focus of therapy, the *terminal objective* behaviorally defines the accomplishment of a goal. While the goal may be stated broadly or in general terms, the objective is always a description of a clearly observable outcome. A *short-term objective* relates to the overall goal, but has a higher probability of being realized in a shorter and more reasonable length of time. "Reasonable" is defined by the individual music therapist, who must consider that achievement of this objective symbolizes a turning point in therapy. Such accomplishments should provide a signal to both therapist and client that successful progress is being made. Additionally, it indicates that an important step toward the *long-term objective* is reached.

The word "long" in long-term must, likewise, be considered by the therapist in light of the particular circumstances surrounding referral, the nature of the problem, and probability of therapeutic success. Thus, long-term may refer to a period of months or, literally, a lifetime. Striving for something in the long-term offers a broad perspective for therapy and an incentive for growth and change throughout therapy and beyond. Short- and long-term objectives define success and specify the point at which it is achieved. Meeting the long-term objectives implies that therapy will cease. As this terminal point in therapy is reached, new directions, or goals and objectives, will be established for future challenges.

Music therapists have an additional task to perform in this process of defining therapeutic aims. Because behavior is observed within a musical context, objectives must be set both for the music therapy setting and outside it, in an environment more natural to the client. An objective may be met in music therapy, but if client behavior fails to generalize beyond the confines of this setting, behavioral change is of limited value. Setting two such objectives ensures that generalization of results is sought as an aim of therapy.

Guidelines for Setting Objectives

Whether writing short- or long-term, music therapy- or generalization-based objectives, the following guidelines may be utilized:

1. Describe observable, measurable behavior: Use words which are easily interpreted and describe what the client "does" rather than "knows" or "understands."
2. Specify a direction of change: Will the behavior be increased, decreased, or maintained, and to exactly what degree? Is there a new skill/behavior to be achieved?
3. Delineate the boundaries: Cite any conditions, specifications, and criteria for success.

Translating goals into specific objectives, the music therapists set the following aims for their work:

For Joshua:
> Long-term Goal: Deinstitutionalization.
> Long-term Objective: To meet all of the criteria specified for placement in community home or facility.

Short-term Goals: Successful completion of vocational training program in sheltered workshop; improvement in fine motor coordination.

Short-term Objective (outside music therapy): To be able to grasp 100% of small objects in container, and place on conveyor belt (on assembly line) within time allotted (as defined).

For Ann:

Long-term Goal: positive social interaction with others outside of own room.

Long-term Objective: To speak with others away from own room, while focusing visually on them for at least 50% of the time.

Short-term Goal: Increase awareness of others.

Short-term Objective (outside music therapy): To maintain visual focus (as defined) on a familiar person's face as that person moves six inches in five different directions.

For Michael:

Long-term Goals: Improved scholastic achievement; elimination of disruptive activity.

Long-term Objectives: To achieve grade level work in all subjects, based on standardized test performance; to eliminate disruptive outbursts.

Short-term Goal: Decreased disruptive activity in the classroom.

Short-term Objective (outside music therapy): To decrease time spent out-of-seat by 50% and increase attention to the task (as per response definition) by 50%.

Case Examples

Let us review the accomplishments of Joshua's, Ann's and Michael's music therapists. A summary of their clinical notes is given for each case.

Joshua

CLIENT: Joshua

LONG-TERM GOAL: Deinstitutionalization.

SHORT-TERM GOAL: Successful completion of the vocational training program in the workshop; improvement in fine motor coordination.

TARGET BEHAVIOR: Grasping small objects (pincer grasp).

RESPONSE DEFINITION: Grasping: Picking up small, thin object (size of a quarter) from a group or box of such objects with the thumb and index finger. The tips of the fingers must be used (any part between the top of the nail and the beginning of the second joint in the finger), and the object must be lifted to eye level and held in place for at least six seconds. If the object shifts its position between the fingers while being held up, even if it is unreleased, this would not represent a correct response. Grasping is recorded as the frequency of correct responses, calculated as a percentage of correct responses out of total attempts.

LONG-TERM OBJECTIVE: To meet all of the criteria specified for placement in group home or community-based facility.

SHORT-TERM OBJECTIVE (outside music therapy): To be able to grasp 100% of small objects in container, and place on conveyor belt (on assembly line) within time allotted (as defined).

SHORT-TERM OBJECTIVE (in music therapy): To lift a pick (autoharp pick) from a box of picks (as per response definition) and strum an autoharp chord for six beats ($\quarternote = 60$).

Ann

CLIENT: Ann

LONG-TERM GOAL: Positive social interaction with others outside of her own room.

SHORT-TERM GOAL: Increased awareness of others.

TARGET BEHAVIOR: Visual focusing on object or person.

RESPONSE DEFINITION: Visual focusing: Having the gaze in both eyes directed toward a specified object or a person's eyes which are located approximately one and one-half feet away. Additionally, when the object or person moves six or more inches, the eyes should shift within two seconds to focus on the new position. Even if the object or person is, at first, directly in front of the eyes, the shift in focus is required to test the response. The eyes need not follow the object or person constantly in its movement, but must locate this new position within two seconds. Focusing is recorded as frequency of appropriate shifts in focus, calculated as a percentage of responses out of total trials. (A trial is defined as a change in position of the stimulus object or eyes by the therapist.)

LONG-TERM OBJECTIVE: To speak with others away from her own room, while focusing visually on them for at least 50% of the time.

SHORT-TERM OBJECTIVE (outside music therapy): To maintain visual focus (as defined) on a familiar person's eyes as that person moves six inches in five different directions. (The person might be a relative, friend, staff member or significant other.)

SHORT-TERM OBJECTIVE (in music therapy): 1) To maintain visual focus (as defined) on a musical instrument or sound source as it is moved six inches in five different directions. 2) To maintain visual focus (as defined) on the music therapist's eyes as the therapist moves six inches in five different directions.

Michael

CLIENT: Michael

LONG-TERM GOALS: Improved scholastic achievement; elimination of disruptive activity.

SHORT-TERM GOAL: Decreased disruptive activity in the classroom.

TARGET BEHAVIOR A: Inappropriate behavior to be decreased — out-of-seat behavior during academic work in classroom.

RESPONSE DEFINITION A: Out-of-seat behavior: The number of seconds spent away from seat or place designated by the teacher for a given academic activity without permission. Out-of-seat means that no part of the body below the waist is touching the seat. The only exception is in the case of standing on the chair which is considered out-of-seat. Kneeling on a chair or placing one leg on the chair is not considered "out-of-seat;" neither is leaving the seat on the teacher's request. (The teacher must specify where the student is required to be during each recording period and the conditions under which the student may leave his place.) The duration of the behavior is recorded, yielding a percentage of seconds out-of-seat during the total observation time.

TARGET BEHAVIOR B: Appropriate behavior to be increased — attention to the task.

RESPONSE DEFINITION B: Attention to the task: The number of seconds spent looking at the teacher or materials specified by her, reading or writing. "Looking at" means visual gaze is focused in the direction of the teacher or materials. Attention to the task includes time engaged in any one of the above activities so that writing is considered a positive response even if the student is looking away from materials. (The teacher must specify the materials required for the lesson.) The duration of the behavior yields a percentage of seconds attending to the task during the total observation period.

LONG-TERM OBJECTIVES: To achieve grade level work in all subjects, based on standardized achievement test performance; to eliminate disruptive outbursts.

SHORT-TERM OBJECTIVE (outside music therapy): To decrease time spent out-of-seat by 50% and increase attention to the task by 50% during academic lessons.

SHORT-TERM OBJECTIVE (in music therapy): To decrease time spent out-of-seat by 50% and increase attention to musical task or therapist (as per response definition) by 50% during sessions.

In the chapter on Assessment, we were introduced to Ralph, the young man who was blinded in an automobile accident. Let us see how Ralph's music therapist established goals and objectives for their work.

Ralph

CLIENT: Ralph

LONG-TERM GOALS: Resumption of regular social activities and positive social behavior.

SHORT-TERM GOALS: Partaking in leisure activities and interacting with others on a regular basis.

TARGET BEHAVIOR A: Participation in activities outside his own room, specifically piano practice and talking with others.

RESPONSE DEFINITION A: Such participation will be operationally defined as the number of minutes spent engaged in each of the following activities: 1) time spent outside his bedroom, 2) time spent at the piano, engaged in playing notes, and 3) time spent talking with others via telephone or in direct communication. Ralph will record total time spent per day on a specially designed chart.

TARGET BEHAVIOR B: Positive statements about self.

RESPONSE DEFINITION B: Positive statements about self include sentences which include a word referring to one's self ("I," "me," or "myself") and an adverb, adjective or noun which implies a positive attribute.

Verbs in present or future tense which also express a positive attitude toward the self may be used in a positive statement, but must modify one's self. In other words, "I can do it!", "I like myself now," or "I will adjust to this" qualify as positive statements, but "I like music," "I used to enjoy life," or "I should be happier than I am" do not meet all criteria for positive statements. Words which are relatively neutral, such as "OK" or "all right," will not qualify as positive adjectives. Examples of positive statements about the self are: "I am getting better," "I feel stronger," "Life is treating me well," "I am a more tolerant person than I was," and "I am a good singer."

LONG-TERM OBJECTIVES: To leave the house on a daily basis; to interact with others in a positive way most of the time.

SHORT-TERM OBJECTIVES: To leave the bedroom for nine hours each day; to practice piano one-half hour per day; to speak with one friend or person about positive things once each day; to increase the rate of unsolicited positive statements about himself to three per music therapy session; to increase the rate of positive statements about himself to once a day.

Conclusions

Identifying goals, target behaviors and objectives is the first step in developing a music therapy treatment plan. In addition to guiding the course of therapy, this process allows the therapist to observe and measure the outcomes of music therapy.

Summary

This chapter offers guidelines for setting goals and objectives and for defining target behaviors. Problems become explicit target behaviors, which are described in detail in response definitions. The definitions make the gathering of quantifiable information possible, thus facilitating an objective evaluation of client change.

Short- and long-term goals are defined more clearly in behavioral objectives. The target behaviors are able to be measured through baseline observations and throughout the course of therapy.

Key Words

Goal
> An expected outcome of therapy; purpose or direction for treatment.

Inter-observer agreement
> A measure of reliability of observers; the degree to which two or more observers concur that specific events or behaviors have occurred.

Long-term goal
> The desired outcome after a considerable period of time.

Long-term objective
> A specific therapeutic aim, stated as a clearly observable outcome, which can be realized after a considerable period of time.

Response definition
> A complete behavioral description of a target behavior, which includes a concise descriptive term, boundaries or limits for the behavior, observational strategies and examples of borderline responses.

Short-term goal
> The desired outcome which is possible to achieve in the near future.

Short-term objective
> A specific therapeutic aim, stated as a clearly observable outcome, which is possible to realize in the near future.

Terminal objective
> The last in a series of short- and/or long-term objectives, specifying the expected outcome or accomplishment of a goal.

References

Alley, J. M. (1979). Music in the IEP: Therapy/Education. *Journal of Music Therapy*, *15*, 111–127.

Levine, E. L., & Wexler, E. M. (1981). *An act of congress.* New York: MacMillan. p. 94–142.

Madsen, C. H., Jr., & Madsen, C. K. (1998). *Teaching/discipline: A positive approach for educational development* (4th ed.). Raleigh, NC: Contemporary Publishing Company of Raleigh.

For Further Reading

Mager, R. F. (1962). *Preparing instructional objectives.* Belmont, CA: Fearon Publishing.

Standley, J. M., & Hughes, J. E. (1996). Documenting developmentally appropriate objectives and benefits of a music therapy program for early intervention: A behavioral analysis. *Music Therapy Perspectives*, *14*, 87–94.

I think and feel in sounds.
—*Maurice Ravel (1875–1937)*

Chapter 7

Observation

A lthough I always considered myself a good observer, I have just begun to nurture a side of me that is mindful as well as observant of my world. Practicing meditation has taught me ways to see more of what is around me. I have taken time to stop and see and hear and feel and touch and taste. It has helped me become a more observant music therapist and I am grateful. I now make sure to take the time to see what is happening in every session. I take time to listen to the music instead of allowing my mind to race ahead to my plans for the next song. I am clear when I am being with the person or the group and when I am stepping back from the process to observe. In this way, I am learning more about the subjective and objective experience of being a music therapist.

This chapter presents observation techniques which allow the therapist to zero in on the target behavior and see what the person is doing, how many times or how long, and some of the surrounding events which may contribute to the nature of this behavior. Systematic observation of the target behavior will reveal the degree to which the behavior is manifest and offer clues for its treatment. It is most desirable to observe both in the music therapy session and in another setting where change is intended. Pre-established behavioral objectives state or imply whether the target behavior is to be increased, decreased or maintained. The response definition states exactly what is to be observed, and whether this behavior is discrete or continuous.

Methods of Recording

Frequency Recording

Discrete events, variables or behaviors have a distinct beginning and ending, and are amenable to being counted as separate responses. A *frequency count* is commonly used to measure the strength of discrete behaviors, and is simply a record of the number of times the behavior occurs. Discrete behaviors which can be counted in this manner include: hitting, inappropriate vocalization, negative statements, chords played correctly on a guitar, words clearly articulated in a song, letters of the alphabet written within boundaries, musical instruments identified by hearing their sounds, and gross movements correctly imitated. These behaviors and others like them can be recorded with devices such as a wrist or grocery counter or with check marks on a piece of paper.

When behaviors are observed within a specific length of time and in a particular context, a response rate or percentage may be calculated and compared across sessions. Often, a response is specifically solicited by a therapist's question, instruction, or structured opportunity. In this case, the therapist's stimulus and the client's response form a pair of "related events." The percentage of desired responses out of the total number of solicitations is calculated. For instance, Joel answered six out of ten questions correctly; Mary Jane imitated eight of the therapist's twelve movements.

Duration Recording

Some behaviors are more continuous in nature, occurring for a certain duration of time. The therapist may be interested in the length of time the behavior lasts rather than whether or not it has occurred. The number of seconds or minutes one maintains eye contact, balances on one foot, sits in a chair, smiles, cries, holds a note on a wind instrument, practices singing, engages in stereotypical rocking behavior, or remains relaxed may be recorded by a *duration recording* technique. A stopwatch is a useful piece of apparatus for timing behaviors, although any time piece will do, as long as the observer is able to quickly record the precise time that the behavior started and stopped.

It should be noted that many behaviors may be either counted or timed, e.g., eye contact, vocalization, disruptive behavior, playing an instrument. By examining the unique nature of the person's behavior, the therapist will decide whether it is most feasible to change the number of responses or the duration of responding. Frequency and duration recording are simple observation techniques. However, not all behaviors are simple to observe, and may require alternative methods.

Interval Recording

Interval time-sampling is a popular observation strategy which is employed when behavior is not clearly discrete. It involves determining whether or not the target behavior has occurred during a brief interval of time (usually about ten seconds). The observer "samples" the behavior under one of the following conditions for recording a response:

1. Individual must respond during entire interval;
2. Individual must respond at some time during interval; or
3. Individual must be responding at the moment of completion of the interval.

Planned Activity Check

A variation on the time-sampling theme, is a *Planned Activity Check*, known as Pla-Check (Hanser, 1980), which requires the observer to record the number of group participants engaged in the target behavior at the end of a pre-determined observation interval. This has obvious advantages in a group music therapy setting, including the ability to record the behavior of more than one individual and to do so with a minimum of disruption to the activities.

To Observe or to Do Therapy

Although much can be learned about behavior through continuous observation, many therapists resist using such rigorous recording techniques. They believe that while recording, their attention must be deflected from client interaction and music leadership. They joke about being able to juggle a guitar, stopwatch and recording sheet with eyes fixed on one or more clients. There is little doubt, however, that behavioral observation is a significant tool for testing the impact of therapy. To allay this concern, time-sampling offers a viable recording option, allowing the therapist to determine a reasonable time frame for observing individuals during the music therapy session. Using variations on interval time-sampling, the therapist chooses a limited time for observation, and selects a separate interval for recording. Behavior is sampled during these pre-determined periods. This minimizes interruptions due to recording, and allows the therapist to maintain full attention on the person or group.

Music therapists have a special advantage when recording. Because musical selections, phrases, verses, measures, and beats divide the passage of time into somewhat equivalent intervals, the structure of a music therapy session provides an automatic time-keeper. The therapist who organizes each session with some consistently similar elements, e.g., activities which provide a fixed number of opportunities for response, songs which have the same number of verses or phrases, or pieces of the same tempo, can use these segments to compare data recorded across sessions. Using music to measure time also frees a hand which might, otherwise, be controlling a stopwatch. Kimberly is able to remain on-task and behave appropriately during four out of five songs; Andrew provides a rhythmic drum beat for 14 out of 16 measures.

Reliable Recording

It must be pointed out that therapists, by the nature of their personal involvement, are highly biased observers. Desirous of a positive therapeutic outcome, therapists are naturally influenced in their observations. To ensure that reliable data are being gathered, a second, independent observer should record target behaviors simultaneously, at least once during different phases of music therapy. A measure of agreement between observers (or inter-observer agreement), known as the *reliability coefficient*, should be calculated to obtain a level of confidence in those data. One convenient method of calculation yields a percentage:

$$\text{Reliability} = \frac{\text{Agreements}}{\text{Agreements} + \text{Disagreements}} \times 100\%$$

where agreements = number or amount of time the target behavior is observed by both; and disagreements = number or amount of time the target behavior is observed by only one observer.

A reliability coefficient of approximately 85% or above is expected on most behavioral measures. Achieving less, the therapist may wish to revise the response definition or implement more precise recording procedures.

Clinical Examples of Recording

Maria

Maria's music therapist is treating her for aphasia. With her speech therapist's help, he has devised an assessment tool to test Maria's ability to say simple words which are printed on flash cards. As the music session immediately follows speech therapy, the therapists have arranged to overlap five minutes so that they may meet together with Maria. The music therapist proceeds to observe the target behavior of "reading words," using the speech therapist as reliability observer. Out of twenty words, ten are recorded as correct by the music therapist. To his surprise, the speech therapist only counts five correct. The reliability coefficient is calculated as Agreements / (Agreements + Disagreements) x 100%, or 5 / (5 + 5) x 100% = 50%, hardly an acceptable level.

Upon discussion, it becomes evident that the music therapist considered any vocal approximation of the word as correct, whereas the speech therapist has defined "correct" as a clear pronunciation of each phoneme in the word on the first attempt. The therapist also realized that he has no information regarding either Maria's eyesight or intellectual functioning level, factors which obviously affect test results. Lack of preparation for assessing the target behavior has caused this therapist some embarrassment.

Keith

In another setting, music therapist, parent and teacher team up to examine the behavior of a physically aggressive 10-year-old, named Keith. The most common form of Keith's aggression is tantrums, which he exhibits at both home and school, at a rate of approximately two per day. Keith's mother reports that she hardly ever has a positive interaction with him since the tantrums began, about six months ago. The music therapist is interested in observing this behavior, but wishes to intervene as soon as possible to treat such a negative behavior.

Mother and teacher assist the music therapist to develop a response definition, a relatively simple task since it is obvious to them when tantrums occur. Mother and father will serve as reliability observers; teacher and classroom aide will also pair up to make independent observations. The music therapist asks them all to record the frequency of tantrums over a three-day period. At the end of this time, they are instructed to deal with tantrums by removing Keith from the room, and ignoring him for the duration of the tantrum.

After one week, the music therapist returns to find out the results of their observations. Tantrums are reported to occur at school once a day except on the fourth day of observation (start of ignoring), when they occur twice. At home, Keith has one tantrum per day for the first three days, then two per day for two days, then one on each of the last two days. The frequency of tantrums has increased on the first days of the ignoring procedure.

However, the observers reveal that the duration of tantrums on the last two days of observation is considerably shorter than they have ever been before.

The music therapist decides to record the duration of tantrums rather than their frequency. While encouraged that the duration of tantrums is already decreasing, the therapist will focus on the incompatible behavior of positive verbal interaction between Keith and parents. Discussions about music, musical games, and Keith teaching his parents new songs will set the stage for such communication. In addition, on days in which no tantrums occur, time for special musical activities of Keith's choice will be set aside in the evening by one or both parents. Parents, teacher and aide will continue to collect data on tantrums throughout treatment.

Baseline Observations

Given the variability of human behavior and its vulnerability to environmental factors, it is wise to observe behavior over a period of time before making assumptions that a true representation of its present level is reflected. A *baseline* is a set of target behavioral observations which is indicative of functioning without therapeutic intervention. Baseline observations are generally displayed on a graph with sessions, trials or days arranged on the abscissa (horizontal line) and data on the target behavior shown on the ordinate (vertical line). Baseline is recorded until a relatively stable level of responding is observed. For a behavior which is to be decreased, the baseline graph may ascend. For a behavior which is to be increased, baseline may descend before treatment procedures commence.

While it is tempting for a therapist to praise a client or implement other behavior change techniques, this tendency must be resisted while recording baseline. Baseline must function as a basis for comparison with later music therapy procedures. Normally, baseline serves as an indication of behavior in the natural environment. Within music therapy, however, it may be desirable to observe target behavior under certain music conditions which may resemble therapeutic ones, but are not designed to affect the target specifically. Observations under this condition may then be compared with those under treatment conditions where a particular music stimulus or therapy technique is added.

This procedure is not truly a baseline-treatment model in the strictest sense; but it enables the therapist to attempt to isolate the added variable and look at its effects upon the target behavior. Such an application has been found valuable by music therapists. In Figure 7.1, noncontingent background music in an initial observation phase is compared with music contingent upon target behavior in a treatment phase (Hanser, 1974). In Figure 7.2, effects of contingent music and art activities are compared with baseline procedures (Miller, Dorow, & Greer, 1974). It is advisable, however, for the therapist not to stray too far afield from the non-treatment aspect of baseline in contrasting conditions and to implement stringent requirements for baseline observations outside of the music therapy setting (see Figures 7.1 and 7.2).

Functional Analysis

Not only is it important to observe the target behavior before implementing a therapeutic program, but it is also helpful to take the opportunity to observe behaviors and conditions surrounding this behavior. A functional analysis of the behavior attempts to do just that. Particularly relevant to an examination of problem behaviors, the functional analysis further attempts to identify environmental events which are maintaining and controlling the problem. It involves an observation of:

1. events which precede the onset of the problem, i.e., antecedent stimuli or *antecedents;*
2. events which immediately follow the problem behavior, i.e., *consequences* which are potentially reinforcing or punishing; and
3. the problem behavior itself, i.e., the frequency or duration of undesirable responding.

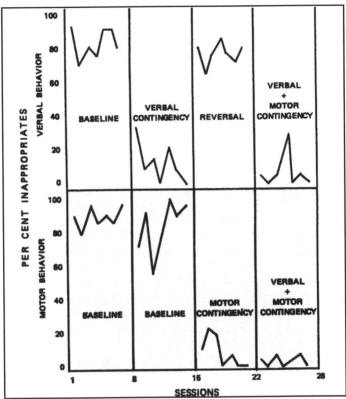

Figure 7.1. Example from music therapy literature:
Reprinted from Hanser (1974), *Journal of Music Therapy*.

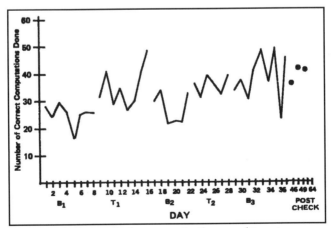

Figure 7.2. Example from music therapy literature:
Reprinted from Miller, Dorow & Greer (1974), *Journal of Music Therapy*.

The functional analysis should be performed in the setting in which the problem behavior has been observed or has occurred. If it is not possible to arrange such a naturalistic observation, then an environment as analogous as possible to the problem situation should be constructed in an attempt to evoke the inappropriate response. If Billy's fights with classmates occur most often on the playground, then bouts of fighting might also be observed within a group of free play activity. There are obvious limitations to staging an environment where not all the characters are present and the background is clearly different. In order to gain a reasonable understanding of the conditions which maintain problematic behavior, there is no viable substitute for direct observation of those stimuli which are operating in the person's environment.

A functional analysis might start with a narrative accounting, also known as an *anecdotal record*, which lists events encountered by the client. The recorder notes distinguishable behavior of the person and relevant others, events or perceptual stimuli which intrude into the environment, i.e., sounds or smells, and any other obvious changes in the surrounding environment. Particular attention is paid to those behaviors which immediately follow the targeted problem as potential sources of reinforcement for that behavior. A review of the narrative record will reveal those events which temporally preceded occurrences of problem behavior. The events may be evoking the inappropriate behavior. When repeated observations of the problem response yield replication of the same antecedents and consequences over time, this will lend greater certainly that these observed events are controlling the problem. Once these contingencies are identified, the therapist may set out a plan for manipulating them in an attempt to change the problem behavior.

The person observed in Figure 7.3 is a child with a behavioral disorder named Warren, who strikes out repeatedly at other children and teachers. An analysis of these observations reveals that the same antecedent behavior, laughing and hitting fists together, precedes the target behavior on every observed occasion. This means that it might be possible to predict or prevent the occurrence of striking out upon observing this antecedent behavior. Secondly, when the consequences of striking out include physical contact with teachers, the target behavior recurs quickly thereafter. After isolation, there is a longer interval before Warren strikes again (see Figure 7.3). By the end of the one and one-half hour observation period, the therapist is prepared to initiate a plan whereby Warren's laughing and hitting of fists together yield immediate isolation from the group. Having identified the critical events surrounding this target behavior, the therapist develops a simple, but effective strategy for eliminating Warren's destructive behavior.

Subjective Observation

The observation techniques presented here are designed to produce objective evidence of the person's progress in therapy. It may be argued that it is the therapist's subjective impressions that make meaning of these data. This less formal analysis of the target behavior and of all other behaviors is a natural part of the therapist's overall evaluation.

DATE: April 29

CLIENT: Warren

BEHAVIOR: Physically striking out with fist(s) at object or person

Time	Antecedent	Target Behavior	Consequence
11:02 AM	laughs, hits fists together	hits Peggy	Staff member pulls him aside, reprimands him
11:05 AM	laughs, hits fists together	hits Peggy	Staff member pulls him aside, holds his hands, says, "No."
11:07 AM	laughs, hits fists together	hits Peggy	Staff member isolates him in corner of room for 3 minutes
11:35 AM	laughs, hits fists together	hits wall	Staff member takes his hands away from wall, holds them and says, "No."
11:40 AM	laughs, hits fists together	hits wall repeatedly	Staff member isolates him in corner for 3 minutes

Figure 7.3. Functional analysis of an institutionalized child's striking out behavior.

The relative value of subjective and objective perspectives is not to be argued here. Perhaps, the most critical issue is for the music therapist to be able to discriminate between subjective and objective data when making decisions about the person and about treatment. Clinical impressions and interpretations are qualitatively different from objective and reliable behavioral observations. Both contribute to a comprehensive perspective on the whole person. It is important to report each type of observation separately, presenting quantitative data and qualitative interpretations. The therapist should identify the source of information for these interpretations, and state how conclusions are drawn.

It goes without saying that music therapists listen to the music. They also hear, observe, sense and perceive what is happening with the person. Sharp intuition and objective data guide clinical work to maximize the potential of every moment in therapy. As they observe, music therapists may ask themselves some questions:

1. When I observe, is there something new or different about the person that I am seeing or sensing at this time? If so, what external factors e.g., medication, incidents, environmental changes, might be contributing?

2. When I listen, what do I hear in the person's music? What do I hear being expressed verbally and nonverbally? Are these perceptions consistent with other observations?

3. When I use my intuition, what do I sense about the person? Is this something that I should check or confirm with the person?

4. When I think about the process, is there something that strikes me about what is happening?

5. Is there anything else that I am perceiving which might call for further investigation?

6. What is my process as an observer? Am I stepping back from the process to observe? Am I paying attention to the person?

7. Am I aware of what I am observing objectively? Am I aware of my interpretations as subjective factors?

These notes comprise subjective information in the process of observation which the therapist may take into account in treatment planning. Therapists may be advised to confer with fellow professionals or family members regarding their potential meaning. Other indications may become evident when these observations yield information about medication side effects or outside circumstances which require action.

Conclusion

Observation offers important clues about the target behavior, but also, about many other factors which are critical to treatment planning. Baseline data, functional analyses and subjective evaluation provide significant sources of information about initial functioning, and contribute to a comprehensive picture of the client at this early stage of therapy.

Summary

Behavioral observation involves several quantitative methods for measuring behavior. Frequency, duration, interval and Planned Activity Check recording provide quantitative data for documenting client progress. There are challenges to observing while doing therapy, but these should not prevent the music therapist from collecting some observational data about the target behavior. To ensure the objectivity of observations, reliability should be calculated by enlisting the help of a second, independent observer. Baseline observations give an indication of the level of the target behavior without therapeutic intervention. A functional analysis provides evidence of the antecedents and consequences of the behavior. Subjective analyses assist in the interpretation of these findings.

Key Words

Anecdotal record
    Narrative account of behaviors and events which is
    recorded while observing.

Antecedents (antecedent stimuli)
Events which precede a behavior, sometimes setting the occasion for an occurrence of the behavior.

Baseline
A record or graph of behavioral observations which are recorded over time and without the application of systematic intervention.

Consequences
Events which follow a behavior, sometimes as the result of the occurrence of the behavior.

Duration recording
An observational recording system in which one notates the length of time a behavior occurs.

Frequency count
An observational recording system in which one notates the number of times a behavior occurs.

Interval time-sampling
An observational recording system in which one notates whether or not a behavior is occurring during a specific interval of time.

Planned Activity Check (Pla–Check)
An observational recording system in which one notates the number of group participants engaged in a target behavior at the end of a predetermined observation interval.

Reliability coefficient
A measure of agreement between observers which may be calculated as the number of agreements between observers divided by the total number of agreements and disagreements, times 100%.

References

Hanser, S. B. (1974). Group-contingent music listening with emotionally disturbed boys. *Journal of Music Therapy, 11*, 113–124.

Hanser, S. B. (1980). *Music therapy practicum: A manual for behavior change through music therapy*. Oakland: Pea Press.

Miller, D. M., Dorow, L. G., & Greer, R. D. (1974). The contingent use of music and art for improving arithmetic scores. *Journal of Music Therapy, 11*, 57–64.

For Further Reading

Bentzen, W. R. (1991). *Seeing young children: A guide to observing and recording behavior*. Florence, KY: Delmar.

Madsen, C. H., Jr., & Madsen, C. K. (1998). *Teaching/discipline: A positive approach for educational development* (4th ed.). Raleigh: Contemporary Publishing.

Suen, H. K. (1989). *Analyzing quantitative behavioral observation data*. Mahwah, NJ: Lawrence Erlbaum.

Sulzer-Azaroff, B., & Mayer, G. R. (1977). *Applying behavior-analysis procedures with children and youth*. New York: Holt, Rinehart and Winston.

Music is the electrical soil in which the spirit lives, thinks and invents.

—*Ludwig van Beethoven (1770–1827)*

Chapter 8

Music Therapy Strategies

Whenever someone new is referred to me for music therapy, I find myself using a new strategy. I select from a variety of instruments, genres, approaches, methods, systems, schools, and philosophies. I wonder at the endless number of possibilities to meet this person musically and therapeutically. Of course, every combination of music plus therapist creates a unique strategy. Each therapist adds a specific personality, history and philosophy to a given music therapy approach, thus modifying it in some way. A presentation of all music therapy strategies would, therefore, be an infinite list.

Rather than attempt a comprehensive identification of music therapy programs, this chapter selects a few of those approaches which are supported by research. These include music as a behavioral consequence, music as an antecedent or cue, teaching music to teach other skills, and music in insight therapy. The chapter also presents maintenance and generalization techniques which ensure that therapy is geared toward making changes beyond the confines of the music therapy setting.

Music as a Behavioral Consequence

Music as Positive Reinforcement

Toby has remained on-task in the music therapy session for the entire activity. He will be the first to lead the group in the next song. Martha finished her workbook assignment before the time allotted. She can spend the rest of the class period listening to music over headphones. When Mark is depressed, he remains in his room at the group home. The music therapist has stipulated that if he will join the group in the dining room for a meal, then the guitar lessons that he has requested will begin.

These examples attest to the potential that music has as a means of *positive reinforcement*. Music listening, instrumental lessons, creative experiences and group music activities are some of the many stimuli which have reinforcing properties and provide incentives for behavioral change. Learning theory teaches that when a behavior results in pleasant consequences, this behavior will continue or increase. When music therapists offer music as a contingency for desirable behavior, they often find that it has the same effect. When it does result in an increase in behavior, it is known as positive reinforcement. There are several rules, however, for dispensing contingent music to reinforce behavior:

1. A clear relationship must be established between the occurrence of a target behavior and its musical consequence. The therapist must specify exactly how and when the music contingency will be administered.

2. The behavior which earns contingent music should have a high probability of occurrence. The process of rewarding *successive approximations* of a terminal behavior is a popular and effective behavioral technique, known as *shaping* (Skinner, 1953).

3. The music consequence should be offered immediately after the occurrence of the specified behavior. If this is not feasible, then a check mark, point, or some other symbol which is later redeemable for music may be substituted when the behavior is completed. Precise rules for the exchange of these points must be designated.

4. There should be a direct, positive relationship between behavioral improvement and the desirability of the musical conse-

quence. The number of correct responses might yield the number of seconds allowed for music listening. Or, a special music privilege might be withheld until a certain behavioral level is maintained. It is preferable that successive approximations yield small increments of desirable musical consequences, so that even the smallest behavioral changes are rewarded in some way.

5. The selected consequence should be available only after the desired response. Providing the consequence consistently is sometimes difficult, but always important. Music as reinforcement is widely documented in the music therapy literature. The scope of its success in different populations, age ranges and clinical settings may be due to the strength of music's appeal to so many people (Hanser, 1983). Thus, it holds tremendous potential for changing an enormous variety of behaviors.

Music as Negative Punishment

Just as the addition of music contingent upon a response often increases that behavior, so too, the contingent withdrawal of music has been known to decrease behavior. When it decreases that behavior effectively, it is known as *negative punishment*. "Punishment" is defined as having resulted in decreased behavior, and "negative" refers to the withdrawal of a stimulus.

Examples of music stimuli used to punish responses include: removing an instrument from a child after hitting a peer; turning off recorded background music in a study hall after a student speaks out of turn; and rescinding the right to take a turn in a group activity after a child leaves the circle without permission.

The same general rules for increasing behavior apply to decreasing behavior with this exception: the music contingency is deleted following the occurrence of undesirable behavior, rather than being added after a desirable response. An admonition is in order to use punishment techniques with constraint. Unless augmented with methods of substituting or increasing other more constructive behaviors, punishment techniques may be of limited value, and in some cases, could be potentially harmful (Madsen, Cotter, & Madsen, 1968). The therapist should ensure that positive behavior change is sought by employing a positive approach whenever possible.

Music as a Group Contingency

This method for changing individual behavior may be employed successfully with more than one person when music is contingent upon the behavior of a group as a whole. Such "music *group contingencies*" have been applied in one of two ways:

1. The behavior of any one individual resulted in a consequence for the entire group. In a study of emotionally disturbed boys, when anyone engaged in off-task behavior, background music was interrupted until appropriate behavior was restored. Off-task behavior decreased dramatically when the music interruption contingency was in effect (Hanser, 1974).

2. The behavior of the group as a whole resulted in a group consequence. A certain noise level in a home economics classroom (Wilson & Hopkins, 1973) and on a bus (McCarty, McElfresh, Rice, & Wilson, 1978; Ritschl, Mongrella, & Presbie, 1972) yielded the cessation of background music. These studies demonstrated behavioral change as a function of the group contingency.

Music as a Behavioral Antecedent

Music as a Cue

Hearing a song which describes a simple hand washing routine, children with developmental disabilities are reminded of the steps they must take to clean their hands (Kramer, 1978). During the hours of labor prior to childbirth, expectant mothers listen to music which cues positive and relaxing associations (Hanser, Larson, & O'Connell, 1983). Listening to music reminiscent of their youth, older adults discuss pleasant memories and experiences influential to their growth.

When music is used as an antecedent stimulus to prompt a particular behavior, it sets the occasion for the anticipated response. There are many processes which are in effect as music *cues* behavior.

The melodic line may provide a cue to teach new skills. Music therapists may set the letters of a child's name to a simple tune, and while leading this personalized song, teach them the correct letter sequence. Here, the melody may be cueing the spoken letters.

Rhythm directs behavior in a similar fashion, but perhaps, even more obviously. It has been said that the very basic organizing and energizing capacity of rhythm is the most significant factor in the therapeutic function of music. Rhythmic cues inform us of when to respond or move and enable us to work together as a group (Gaston, 1968). It may be this element that serves to unite us as we behave musically. It is additionally theorized that the repetitious rhythm of the lullaby is responsible for its sleep-inducing effects. Perhaps, too, it is the tempo and rhythm of back-ground music which affects our buying behavior as consumers in a supermarket, our concentration while studying, and our activity level in a commercial establishment with piped-in auditory stimuli. The rhythms which allow us to move together in dance are probably responsible for much of the success of music in perceptual-motor programs where awareness of the body in space and its movement over time is the primary goal.

Harmony, too, prompts certain behavior. We often associate major keys and resolved cadences with pleasant and comforting feelings. Dissonant chords, minor modes, and unresolved dominant seventh chords provoke less pleasant or questioning feelings. The effects of these elements of music are immensely more complex than predictable. The musical prescription to evoke happiness and peace is, and will always be, impossible to define, due to the number of factors which influence human taste and behavior. It is up to the music therapist to manipulate melodic, rhythmic, and harmonic elements, taking into account individual needs and observed effects of different music.

The idea of presenting a stimulus to cue a certain response is central to the learning process. In fact, at the foundation of language acquisition is the simple "*paired-associate*," where the presentation of a single word is a stimulus for the recall of a second word. Music has been a useful adjunct to learning paired-associates, and thus, holds great potential as a cue in short-term memory tasks (Shehan, 1981). *Melodic intonation therapy*, a variation on the musical cue theme, has also achieved success (Krauss & Galloway, 1982; Sparks, Helm, & Albert, 1974, Popovici, 1995).

Another way to look at the musical stimulus is in the actual conditioning of a desired response. When music is used as a *discriminative stimulus*, a response is conditioned to occur in its presence and not to occur in the presence of other stimuli. The individual learns to discriminate between stimuli, and behaves as conditioned. In this way, pregnant women learn to relax in response to hearing selected pieces of music. The practice of relaxation techniques is paired with background music which already cues positive and soothing associations. After repeated rehearsal during pregnancy, music is introduced to the laboring woman in an attempt to produce relaxing musculature as well as ideas and images. A similar conditioning procedure may be applied for anxiety reduction in others, such as pre-operative hospitalized patients (Chetta, 1981) and dental patients (Hanser, Martin, & Bradstreet, 1982).

It is also this phenomenon which may allow music to bring about such responses as increased vocalizations and spontaneous smiling in the infant. Yet, the observed influence of music as early in life as in utero (Bench, 1968) leads one to question when a response to music is actually learned. Its ability to appeal to the very young and serve as a stimulus for a variety of new behaviors demonstrates the remarkable potential that music holds as a therapeutic agent.

In nearly every application of music to affect behavior, it may be said to serve as a cue for an identifiable response. There is a myriad of methodology, however, for developing specific behaviors. Some of the more popular strategies are presented here.

Teaching Music to Teach Other Skills

Several of the examples in this book have illustrated how music teaches non-music skills. This section addresses how music is used to teach academic, perceptual-motor and certain social skills.

There are various principles at work in the application of music to program skill development:

1. Academic subject matter can be taught through musical subject matter. When learning to read music, one is applying the knowledge of translating symbols across a page from left to right. While clapping a rhythmic pattern, one is using simple mathematics to divide a measure into beats. Writing musical notes requires that the notation remain between identifiable boundaries. These examples of notation alone indicate the complementary nature of music and non-music learning.

2. *Musical involvement necessitates the practice of a continuum of skills, particularly in auditory discrimination, perceptual-motor acuity and speech development.* Singing and playing wind instruments involves proper usage of breath control and articulation. Varying degrees of fine motor coordination are required to play musical instruments. Increasing one's vocal range and improving intonation have obvious advantages in developing language. Rhythmic training holds potential for fostering movement with fluidity and regularity. There are innumerable skills employed in making music, and the incentive of working towards a musical product holds great merit for inspiring learning.

3. *Music allows the student to experience academic learning in another dimension.* There are many songs, dances, and musical games of childhood which reiterate basic skills such as counting ("Ten Little Indians"), body awareness and directionality ("Hokey-Pokey"), and knowledge of animals ("Old MacDonald Had a Farm"). Experiencing concepts, particularly

abstract ones like up-down, loud-soft, and long-short, may aid the process of learning, to the point of having children "internalize" these ideas (Reichard & Blackburn, 1973).

4. *Learning music often results in positive psycho-social and emotional changes.* Achieving a musical goal, such as performing or composing a piece of music, can bring an inordinate sense of pride to an individual. Enhanced self-esteem is a common by-product of such an experience. Further, expressing one's self through music is a way of fulfilling the creative potential that each person holds. As has been indicated, positive involvement in musical activity is incompatible with many inappropriate behaviors. After mastering certain musical skills, options for leisure time activities increase to include community-based groups, ensembles and various social activities.

5. *Music provides a structure within which there is freedom* (Gaston, 1968). Music is organized sound in time (Bernstein & Picker, 1966). While it is a highly structured art form, it accommodates individual interpretation and creativity. While an entire group of people are engaged in a musical activity, no two are expressing themselves in precisely the same way. Thus, it provides a format for learning about one's own unique manner of approaching the creative process, expressing one's self, interacting with others, and organizing and interpreting artistic material.

Obviously, while teaching music, one is teaching much more. The subject matter of music, after all, involves the unique interaction of the person with the creative medium. When teaching music to teach other skills, certain guidelines should be considered.

Guidelines for Instructional Music Sessions

1. *Start with music.* Display the musical product of the day's session, when practical. Sing the song to be learned, demonstrate the musical instrument(s) to be used, dance

the dance, play a composition written by another group, listen to a recording identifying themes of the session, or simply state the objective for the day's activities.

2. *Set musical objectives to complement non-music objectives.* Music as well as non-music skills will be learned in the session. List two sets of objectives, citing target behaviors and associated musical outcomes, e.g., playing "Hot Cross Buns" on flutophone and blowing a steady stream of air out of the mouth for six seconds; singing the letters of one's name in song and spelling it upon request. Define successive approximations of the terminal music objective just as you did with non-music behaviors.

3. *Start at the individual's level.* You have already assessed the person's functioning. Refer to the musical assessment profile to determine the present level of musical skills, and keep both in mind as you begin.

4. *Devise an instructional program with small increments of new learning.* Guarantee success by ensuring that one step is mastered before proceeding to the next step. Teach skills of successive difficulty or complexity one by one, introducing a small amount of new learning, and building upon the behaviors already demonstrated. Provide an aesthetically pleasing product at each step, e.g., a song requiring only one note, then two and three notes.

5. *Reward learning appropriately.* Provide incentives for learning by offering approval or other rewards contingent upon progress.

6. *Model when possible.* Demonstrate the music behavior by doing rather than telling. Use other group members as well as yourself to model appropriate music behaviors.

7. *Prompt physically or verbally.* When an individual has difficulty performing the desired task, additional hints or prompts may be called for. To assist in answering a ques-

tion, the initial sound of the answer may be provided by the therapist. A person may require physical guidance in order to respond. The therapist may intervene by actually moving the person in the appropriate manner. When prompts fail to produce the desired response, one should revert to successive approximations of the behavior. Repeated failure requires the therapist to change the instructional strategy or the successive approximations.

8. *Include familiar and simple as well as challenging new music experiences.* Perform music which can be met with success. Repeat activities which have been mastered already to instill confidence and pride. Practice may also "make perfect," but it should not be overused or abused to the point of becoming aversive or boring.

9. *Select music reflecting interest, performance capability, and relevance.* Criteria for the selection of music could include: age and functioning level; familiarity or interest in the music; variety in style, medium and manner of musical involvement; ability to perform, understand or experience it; and the probability of encountering this type of music again (being familiar to peers or family, hearing it on radio, singing it on holidays, etc.).

10. *End each session with music.* Emphasize the musical learning which has been accomplished by ending with a performance or experience which is a culmination of newly-acquired skills.

Music Involvement as Incompatible Behavior

The ability of music to capture a person's attention and guide one's movements in time has been the subject of extensive study. Active music participation often necessitates the use of mind and body in a clearly specified manner. The natural structure of the musical form can be varied by the therapist to encourage associated behavioral changes. For instance, a group of hyperactive children can begin with a circle activity in which they hold hands and follow the leader's movements to music.

Later, they may drop hands, watch and listen, as one child initiates a movement expressing an original interpretation. This therapist is attempting to increase "self-discipline" by phasing out the physical requirements of the activity and gradually offering more opportunities to move freely.

At another level, musical involvement may be a substitute for less acceptable social behavior during leisure time. Individuals who abuse substances or are juvenile offenders might express their needs and obtain gratification through musical involvement. Yet to be tested on a large scale, this idea seems to hold potential, particularly for the adolescent to whom music is a strong influence.

To state that positive involvement with music is incompatible with inappropriate social behavior may be underestimating its impact. In correctional facilities and other settings where the development of trust between client and therapist is a major obstacle, a shared musical experience may open doors to rapport. While engaged in musical activities, the process of trust-building is initiated. At a large state prison, one recreation area is set aside for music therapy. Inmates are free to select from guitars, drum sets and other percussion instruments. A group of instrumentalists have begun to improvise or "jam" together on a regular basis. The music therapist joins in, but allows the group to set the key and rhythm, only offering occasional feedback. After four sessions, two of the musicians begin to discuss their respective predicaments and hopes for the future. They note the importance of having the opportunity to be themselves and express themselves in the jam sessions. They clearly sense that the music therapist understands this, and is worthy of their trust. In subsequent sessions, a greater segment of time is devoted to talking about their changing self-concepts and plans upon release. Music therapy has not only provided a positive, expressive medium but a supportive, trusting environment for working out solutions to life's problems.

Music Education Techniques
Music therapists also employ techniques of music education in their work. Music therapists borrow educational methodologies

to structure their sessions and activities to suit the needs of their clients. Of the many approaches which are applied in the music therapy setting, some deserve special attention.

Orff–Schulwerk, the approach developed by Carl Orff, offers musical activities which emphasize natural rhythms, speech as the basis for song, and exploration in movement and play to encourage creativity and imagination. The rondo form, emphasized by Bitcon as a structure for clinical music therapy, allows the freedom of individual response within a framework of shared group experience (Bitcon, 1976; Hollander & Juhrs, 1974). Zoltan Kodaly's concepts of rhythmic counting and hand signals in sight-singing comprise another experimental scheme for learning about music (Chosky, 1984). Similarly, Suzuki's methodology in teaching instruments to the very young is becoming popular among music therapists (Suzuki, 1981). Mary Helen Richards' "Threshold to Music" series is another set of materials which may be useful in developing musical skills (Richards, 1971). As the aesthetic needs of handicapped students gain greater recognition and importance, more resources for music in special education become available.

New advances in music technology and electronic music have made music and music instruction accessible to virtually everyone. Nonverbal individuals with severe physical limitations are capable of participating in music ensembles using software such as "Switch Ensemble" (Adams, 1998). Adaptive technology has allowed children and adults with special needs to participate actively in creating and performing music they once only could experience passively (Krout, 1987; Krout, Burnham, & Moorman, 1993).

Music in Insight Therapy

In the psychotherapeutic setting, music has been employed as an expressive therapy, (Feder & Feder, 1981), and in *insight therapy* with an emphasis on the projection of feelings through musical experience. Well-documented affective responses to music are at the source of this therapeutic attempt to evoke, express and understand one's own feelings and emotions. The arousal of emotions by music is meant to lead to a fuller self-awareness, which in turn precipitates a heightened perception of one's self. This process attempts to foster insight as a therapeutic goal.

Insight-oriented music therapy has been identified as a viable approach which may follow either reeducative or reconstructive directions (Wheeler, 1983). In *reeducative therapy*, self-growth through readjustment or behavioral change is sought, while *reconstructive therapy* focuses on the reorganization of the personality. As emotions become accessible through musical projection, they are discussed in an attempt to gain greater understanding. The element of insight is brought into play after feelings are identified through listening to music, composing music, improvising, performing, moving to, or talking about music. In reconstructive therapy, unconscious material and deep-set emotions comprise the raw data for therapy.

In an attempt to locate these inner states, music therapists have used guided imagery (Bonny & Savary, 1973) and improvisation (Nordoff & Robbins, 1972) among other techniques. Achieving awareness in an altered state of consciousness is the goal of Guided Imagery and Music (GIM). Specially selected music evokes a client's deep imagery which is verbally processed with the therapist. Therapeutic practice of these and other reconstructive techniques is limited, however, to those who have advanced and specialized training in the area. Research evidence is beginning to be gathered on therapeutic effects of imagery, and this field has gained greater attention in recent years (Bonny, 1994; Sheikh, 1983).

Clinical improvisation or improvisation therapy tends to focus on awareness, nonverbal communication and expression, and integration of self. Improvisational interactions are analyzed as intra- or intermusical, and intra- or interpersonal (Bruscia, 1987). There are many approaches to improvisation, including Creative Music Therapy (Nordoff & Robbins, 1972), Analytical Music Therapy (Priestley, 1994) and Free Improvisation (Alvin & Warwick, 1994).

Philosophical approaches to music therapy are as numerous and diversified as they are to psychotherapy in general (Prochaska & Norcross, 1999). Music therapy procedures have been applied with success to a variety of schools of thought including *Transactional Analysis* (Arnold, 1975), *Rational Emotive Therapy* (Maultsby, 1977), *Behavior Therapy* (Hanser, 1983), and *Psychodynamic Therapy* (Tyson, 1981). *Psychiatric Musicology* is another model which uses music as a metaphor for examining relationships (Stein, 1973). This projective aspect of music has also been addressed in a number of papers (Van den Daele, 1967), although substantiating research is limited, to date.

Clinical Examples

The Crisis Intervention Center strives to create a supportive environment where individuals develop an understanding of their problems and ways to deal with them. Individuals are frequently asked to select a musical recording which describes the way they feel. The group listens to the piece, and then discusses their perceptions of its meaning. In one such music therapy session, Carlos is reticent to participate. He claims that he does not know how he feels, and does not wish to peruse the record collection. The music therapist suggests that Carlos improvise a song on the bass xylophone. Shrugging, he examines the instrument for a few seconds, and then begins a loud, pulsing beat on the lowest note. A delicate, flowing melody enters against this ostinato pattern. At its close, group members cheer, exclaiming about the heartbeat of the music. Then, they interpret: "That is your music, Carlos, private, pensive, but with a healthy heartbeat. It sounds sad, but not confused. The melody knows where it is going." Carlos cannot help but smile. "Maybe, I am more together than I think," he says.

The In-patient Psychiatric Unit of a large hospital is the home of a more dysfunctional group of people. The music therapist structures sessions for groups here in a much more controlled manner. At the start of one session, everyone is encouraged to sing along or accompany a familiar song on one of many percussion instruments. The songs are selected on the basis of life themes to which everyone can relate. After singing "Home on the Range," the group discusses the meaning of "home," their own home situations, and criteria for hospital release in order to return home. Singing serves as a warm-up for such sharing, providing material about a subject on which individuals may project their own experience. As a function of this indirect method, factors such as conditions at home, which may have bearing on the clinical problem, are able to be presented and discussed in an atmosphere of common concern and security.

In a very different setting, people are not referred for any specific problem. Rather, the Senior Community Center has contracted for the services of a music therapist. Groups of local residents meet with the music therapist weekly in an attempt to distract them from somatic complaints and focus on "feeling good." In a Guided Imagery and Music session, the group relaxes to slow, arhythmic sounds of a harp. All are instructed to let the music take them wherever they wish to go. The music therapist guides them on a journey to a wondrous place where all cares and concerns do not exist. Slowly, bringing them back to reality, the therapist asks if anyone met someone they knew or saw a familiar scene. They discuss the images which came to mind with the music, sources of comfort or relaxation along the way, and where in their bodies they felt most and least relaxed.

These examples may demonstrate an extremely indirect method of developing insight or solving problems. Working through the metaphor of musical experience could be considered superfluous in the therapeutic process, especially since any changes realized in this setting must transfer to other aspects of life. Yet, emotions, difficult to access cognitively, are so easily evoked by this nonverbal creative medium. Most music therapy sessions of this kind include techniques to induce awareness and expression of the psycho-social and emotional substance of one's personality or behavior.

Guidelines for Music in Insight Therapy

The organization of a typical music therapy session might be likened to the Sonata form in music. The following is an outline for its format. The words in parentheses correspond with the sections of Sonata form.

1. Warm-ups (Introduction): Success-oriented, nonthreatening activities designed to prepare individuals for sessions, e.g.,
   a. introduction of participants, objectives, and/or materials (music) to be used;
   b. information sharing of participants regarding their present state or recent progress;
   c. physical or musical exercises to prepare for requirements of activities to be performed later;
   d. trust-building exercises to demonstrate the supportive environment (taking small risks by attempting to sing or perform along with others); and
   e. assessment of pre-session feelings and behaviors through projection (How does this music make you feel?) or observation (verbal and nonverbal behaviors demonstrating anxiety).

2. Awareness Activities (Exposition): Experiences which allow participants to explore and become aware of present states, e.g.,
   a. passive music activities which allow for introspection (music listening and Guided Imagery and Music);
   b. nonverbal exercises which encourage individual responses to music (pairs of people mirroring body movements to music);
   c. projective music experiences which allow the participants to express themselves on an instrument or through a music experience which relates similar states;
   d. a musical problem or choice situation designed as a metaphor for similar problem-solving tests;

e. participation in an active musical experience to generate affective responses; and

f. a music learning situation set up to teach new skills and reinforce social behaviors.

3. Affective Activities (Development): Opportunities to examine responses to the Awareness Activities and express this new understanding in a different dimension, e.g.,

a. following passive music activities with active music making or moving to express nonverbal interpretations of the experiences;

b. following nonverbal exercises with verbal or nonverbal activities which use a different musical medium to communicate reactions (such as a musical conversation on two percussion instruments to express the mirroring interaction);

c. interpretation of a projective music experience by the therapist, individual and/or group, pointing out observations and perceptions of the event;

d. discussion of choices made or problem-solving strategies used in such an activity, and opportunities to try out alternatives;

e. further development of affective responses to music through the exploration of contrasting musical stimuli and associated responses;

f. performance of new music skills learned in the session; and

g. feedback from the therapist, individual and/or group sources, identifying responses to any of the music experiences.

4. Synthesis (Recapitulation): Attempts at bringing together awareness, expression, nonverbal/verbal and introspective/projective elements of the music experience, e.g.,

a. an original musical composition to express what has transpired in the session;

b. discussion of the meaning of the experience or perceptions at this point;

    c. conclusions based on projective information, presented for interpretation by individuals;

    d. an analysis of observed strategies and alternatives, applying the musical metaphor to other problem situations;

    e. exploration of affective responses to nonmusical stimuli;

    f. evaluation of the musical and nonmusical outcomes of a music learning experience and analogies to other aspects of life; and

    g. responding to a recording of expressive musical behavior generated during the session.

5. Closure (Coda)

    a. musical or nonmusical summary of the session by therapist and/or participants;

    b. description of progress or process at the end of the session;

    c. performance of music or musical experience which builds upon previously learned music skills or activities;

    d. repeat of the warm-up activity to highlight differences in behavior as a function of the session;

    e. assessment of post-session feelings using the same technique used at start of session; and

    f. assignments given to participant(s) to apply new learning to future situations.

The composer uses Sonata form and knowledge of harmony, instrumentation and other elements to create a beautiful piece of music. So, too, the music therapist brings a multitude of therapeutic and musical arts to this format to bring about changes in people's lives.

The Best Music Therapy Strategy

The preceding presentation of music therapy strategies offers but a glimpse into the therapeutic uses of music. Those approaches which were discussed have the most extensive documentation behind them. However, the success of any music therapy program is dependent upon the impact of the therapist as well as the music. To this combination is added a given philosophical orientation and the therapist's musical talents and skills, creating a unique form of music therapy. Of course, a given therapist has an inordinate number of options in choosing an appropriate strategy and musical medium. How, then, is the best course of action decided?

One important criterion is the database supporting a music therapy technique. The procedures which have been shown to be most effective with similar clinical problems will, most likely, bring success. Yet, every individual presents a new challenge, calling for the adaptation of existing methods and the development of new ones. The model provided in this book enables the music therapist to pursue new directions and sample various approaches with the confidence that their impact can be determined at any point in time. Experimentation with therapeutic strategies will not only identify the most effective one for a particular case, but also contribute to the general body of knowledge in the field.

Maintenance and Generalization Strategies

A group of chronic asthmatic and emphysematic patients are learning controlled, rhythmic breathing techniques with the aid of music therapy. Music of a specific tempo is played as an accompaniment to the exercises. As the patients master breathing in strict time to the music, the musical recording is turned off and patients are asked to silently recall the melodies as they continue to breathe appropriately. In subsequent sessions, music is introduced at the start of the exercise and then, only sporadically. Reminders are given to subvocalize rhythmic tunes in the session and during practice at home. Later, even these are phased out, as the patients develop an appropriate and relaxed breathing pattern without such aids.

In an individual music therapy session with Sybil, her mother and sister are called in to participate. Sybil is said to have emotional difficulties contributing to lack of concentration on school work and inability to get along with her family. The group of three are given homework assignments, e.g., directives to engage in pre-bedtime music listening games in which all three are asked to interact positively about the music and each other. The child's teacher is also included in a session where she is taught a collection of songs by Sybil and the therapist. Back in the regular classroom, when Sybil completes daily academic assignments in the allotted time, she will be able to choose one of her favorite songs as the closing activity of the day. As Sybil begins to complete assignments consistently, this privilege will be given periodically, instead of on a continuous basis.

Paul worked with a music therapist while at the County Detention Center for Youth Offenders. Now, while Paul attends a follow-up Probation Program, the music therapist continues to meet with him. He escorts Paul to a local coffee house where new artists are introduced nightly in performance. While in music therapy, Paul learned several popular songs, and composed pieces which he arranged for guitar and sang quite competently. The therapist encourages Paul to continue to use this newly-discovered talent. He also takes him to a community chorus rehearsal where Paul meets some old high school friends. He appreciates the rich sounds of such a large group singing music he has only sung alone. In periodic telephone conversations, the therapist learns that Paul is continuing these activities on his own and has begun guitar study with the teacher recommended by the therapist.

Fading

The patients with respiratory illnesses undergoing music therapy are developing independence from the therapy setting. Through *fading* (Johnson & Zinner, 1974), the musical stimulus is phased out, enabling the patients to maintain the prescribed breathing type in the absence of background music. Fading procedures involve the gradual removal of controlling stimuli while allowing more naturally occurring stimuli to take over. Musical stimuli may be presented less and less frequently as non-music cues are gradually increased in a typical fading scheme. Children with sensory-motor impairments move across the room to full music accompaniment, then to a drum beat, and then, without any background sounds. In a singing-spelling program, the teacher gives fewer and fewer verbal prompts and fades out the melody until each child spells the target word correctly without any music. A piece is taught on the trumpet with physical guidance first, then with the aid of verbal instruction alone, and finally without the written page of music to cue the correct notes. These situations exemplify uses of fading in the music setting.

Changing Schedules of Reinforcement

To promote maintenance of behaviors increased through reinforcement programs, reinforcing stimuli may be phased out in a similar fashion. After every response is rewarded (continuous reinforcement), a partial reinforcement schedule should be introduced as soon as possible. This means that reinforcers will be dispersed less frequently or will require a greater number of responses before becoming available. In most cases, a variable *schedule of reinforcement* will be most desirable, as is evident from observing cases of slot machine gambling, where the payoff is forthcoming on a variable and unpredictable timetable. The major purpose behind changing the reinforcement schedule, however, is to allow reinforcers in the natural environment to take control over the maintenance of the behavior, while supplanting the reinforcers contrived in the therapy plan.

Other Generalization Techniques

Sybil is fortunate to have aspects of her natural environment, namely her mother, sister and teacher, partake in the music therapy program. Although Sybil seems to be gaining a better understanding of her feelings and attitudes towards family and peers while in music therapy, her behavior at home and at school have not improved significantly. The music therapist wisely incorporates elements closely related to the problem in the therapeutic plan. The interactive "homework" will not only deal with the targeted problem more directly, but also promote *generalization* of behavioral changes which have occurred within therapy sessions. The teacher's involvement will facilitate greater consistency and thoroughness in the handling of Sybil's problem. Note also the therapist's use of song which can be easily learned and enjoyed by Sybil's classmates.

Although not many elements of Paul's home environment were brought into therapy, the music therapist worked specifically to facilitate Paul's transition into the community. Because the musical material employed in therapy was relevant to that available through social and cultural resources, Paul was ready to use the skills he developed in music therapy upon release from the detention center. Encouragement, in the form of telephone prompts, helped maintain personal confidence as well as the continued use of music as a positive expressive outlet for Paul.

Music is not only able to initiate behavioral changes, but also to influence our actions over a longer term. Music can be an effective therapeutic strategy, and like other methods, can be phased out, or faded, to ensure maintenance of behaviors when music is not present. Unlike many other approaches, however, music therapy builds new skills and opportunities whereby the therapeutic agent becomes an ever more important lifetime influence. Music is an important part of a repertoire of coping and survival mechanisms.

Conclusions

The field of music therapy is young. New techniques are still being discovered, undergoing experimentation, and beginning to be reproduced across various populations. Applications to and interactions with other types of therapy have not been addressed in this text, although they, too, represent important innovations in the allied health professions. The explosion of technology will enable anyone to interact with music in the twenty-first century.

It is the music therapist's job to use the same creativity that they nurtured so well in others to individualize and adapt existing music therapy strategies and design new and different methodologies. Let this chapter serve as a point of departure and source of encouragement for the therapist to develop new prototypes for music therapy.

Summary

This chapter presents an overview of music therapy strategies based on research evidence of their effectiveness. Music has been used as a behavioral consequence when employed as positive reinforcement, negative punishment, or as a group contingency. Some interesting work has been done in the area of conditioning new music reinforcers. Used as a cue to set the occasion for a certain response, music is also an effective behavioral antecedent. Additionally, while learning music, people develop many different skills. While involved in musical activities, they cannot perform socially unacceptable behaviors which are incompatible. Music education and technology are making music accessible to everyone, regardless of limitation. Insight-oriented music therapy, whether reeducative or reconstructive, is another approach which focuses on music as an expressive medium. Music has been applied to a variety of psychotherapeutic theories as well. But, no matter how effective the music therapy, an effort must be made to maintain changes observed in therapy and generalize them outside of the therapy setting. Strategies to meet this end include fading, changing schedules of reinforcement, and directly influencing the person's environment.

Key Words

Behavior therapy (applied behavior analysis, behavior modification)
> Therapeutic intervention designed to change behavior using techniques of operant and respondent conditioning as well as behavior analysis.

Cue (stimulus, prompt)
> An event which sets the occasion for a certain behavior to occur.

Discriminative stimulus

A cue which results in a response when that response occurs only after its presentation, and not after other cues.

Fading

The gradual removal of explicit prompts or cues in an attempt to maintain the behavior on its own.

Generalization

The transfer of effects to other behaviors, stimuli, conditions or settings.

Group contingencies

Consequences for a group as a whole dependent upon the occurrence of specified behavior in the entire group.

Insight therapy

An approach to psychotherapy whose objective is awareness of causes or motivation for behavior which, then, leads to control over the behavior and improvement of one's condition.

Melodic intonation therapy

Clinical use of melodies which emphasize intonation in normal speech to develop language skills in aphasic patients and others requiring remediation in propositional language.

Negative punishment

The removal of a stimulus, resulting in a decrease in behavior, e.g., stopping the music after the occurrence of inappropriate behavior which results in a decrease of inappropriate behavior.

Orff-Schulwerk

An approach to music education by Carl Orff which emphasizes creative experience, natural abilities and sounds, the pentatonic scale and ostinati patterns.

Paired-associate

The presentation of one word as a stimulus for the recall of a second word.

Positive reinforcement
The presentation of a stimulus, resulting in an increase in the behavior it follows, e.g., practicing piano increases when the purchase of a new piano is made contingent upon greater practice time.

Psychiatric musicology
A music therapy approach which uses music as a metaphor for examining relationships.

Psychodynamic therapy
A system of psychotherapy based on an individual's unconscious motivation and past experience.

Rational emotive therapy
A system of psychotherapy proposed by Albert Ellis which attempts to confront one's rational belief system as a method of solving problems.

Reconstructive therapy
One type of insight-oriented therapy which examines unconscious and deep-set emotions in order to restructure the personality.

Reeducative therapy
One type of insight oriented therapy which promotes self growth and adjustment through behavior change.

Schedule of reinforcement
The behavioral requirements for a reinforcing stimulus to be delivered. Schedules may be fixed or variable, based on interval or ratio criteria.

Shaping
A technique for developing new behaviors by reinforcing successive approximations of the desired behavior.

Successive approximations
Behaviors which gradually resemble the target behavior or terminal objective.

Transactional analysis
A system of psychotherapy proposed by Eric Berne which examines interactions in terms of explicit roles and games as a method of recognizing and understanding these patterns of behavior.

References

Alvin, J., & Warwick, W. (1994). *Music therapy for the autistic child*. New York: Oxford University.

Adams, J. (1998). *Switch ensemble*. Boston, MA: Switch-In-Time.

Arnold, M. (1975). Music therapy in a transactional analysis setting. *Journal of Music Therapy, 12*, 104–120.

Bench, J. (1968). Sound transmission to the human fetus through the maternal abdominal wall. *Journal of Genetic Psychology, 13*, 85–87.

Bernstein, M., & Picker, M. (1966). *An introduction to music*. Englewood Cliffs, NJ: Prentice-Hall.

Bitcon, C. H. (1976). *Alike and different: The clinical and educational use of Orff-Schulwerk*. Santa Ana, CA: Rosha.

Bonny, H. L. (1994). Twenty-one years later: A GIM update. *Music Therapy Perspectives, 12*, 70–74.

Bonny, H., & Savary, L. M. (1973). *Music and your mind: Listening with a new consciousness*. New York: Harper & Row.

Bruscia, K. E. (1987). *Improvisational models of music therapy*. Springfield, IL: Charles C. Thomas.

Chetta, H. D. (1981). The effect of music and desensitization on preoperative anxiety in children. *Journal of Music Therapy, 18*, 74–84,

Chosky, L. (1984). *The Kodaly method: Comprehensive music education from infant to adult*. Englewood Cliffs, NJ: Prentice-Hall.

Feder, E., & Feder, B. (1981). *The expressive arts therapies*. Englewood Cliffs, NJ: Prentice-Hall.

Gaston, E. T. (1968). *Music in therapy*. New York: MacMillan.

Hanser, S. B. (1974). Group-contingent music listening with emotionally disturbed boys. *Journal of Music Therapy, 11*, 220–225.

Hanser, S. B. (1983). Music therapy: A behavioral perspective. *Behavior Therapist, 6*, 5–8.

Hanser, S. B., Larson, S. C., & O'Connell, A. S. (1983). The effect of music on relaxation of expectant mothers during labor. *Journal of Music Therapy, 20,* 50–58.

Hanser, S. B., Martin, P., & Bradstreet, K. (1982). The effect of music on relaxation of dental patients. Paper presented to the National Conference of the National Association for Music Therapy, Baltimore, MD.

Hollander, F. M., & Juhrs, P. D. (1974). Orff-Schulwerk: An effective treatment tool with autistic children. *Journal of Music Therapy, 11,* 1–12.

Johnson, J. M., & Zinner, C. C. (1974). Stimulus for fading and schedule learning in generalizing and maintaining behaviors. *Journal of Music Therapy, 11,* 84–86.

Kramer, S. A. (1978). The effects of music as a cue in maintaining handwashing in preschool children. *Journal of Music Therapy, 15,* 136–144.

Krauss, T., & Galloway, H. (1982). Melodic intonation therapy with language delayed apraxic children. *Journal of Music Therapy, 14,* 102–113.

Krout, R. (1987). Information sharing: The microcomputing music therapist: A primer. *Music Therapy Perspectives, 4,* 64–67.

Krout, R., Burnham, A., & Moorman, S. (1993). Computer and electronic music applications with students in special education: From program proposal to progress evaluation. *Music Therapy Perspectives, 11,* 28–31.

Madsen, C. K., Cotter, V., & Madsen, C. H., Jr. (1968). A behavioral approach to music therapy. *Journal of Music Therapy, 5,* 70–75.

Maultsby, M. C. (1977). Combining music therapy and rational behavior therapy. *Journal of Music Therapy, 14,* 89–97.

McCarty, B. C., McElfresh, C. T., Rice, S. V., & Wilson, S. J. (1978). The effect of contingent background music on inappropriate bus behavior. *Journal of Music Therapy, 15,* 150–156.

Nordoff, P., & Robbins, C. (1972). *Therapy in music for handicapped children.* New York: St. Martin's.

Popovici, M. (1995). Melodic intonation therapy in the verbal decoding of aphasics. *Romanian Journal of Psychiatry, 33,* 57–97.

Priestley, M. (1994). *Essays on analytical music therapy.* Phoenixville, PA: Barcelona.

Prochaska, J. O., & Norcross, J. C. (1999). *Systems of psychotherapy* (4th ed.). Pacific Grove, CA: Brooks/Cole.

Reichard, C. L., & Blackburn, D. B. (1973). *Music based instruction for the exceptional child.* Denver: Love.

Richards, M. H. (1971). *Language arts through music: A trilogy.* Portola, CA: Richards Institute of Music Education and Research.

Ritschl, C., Mongrella, J., & Presbie, R. (1972). Group time-out from rock and roll music on out-of-seat behavior of handicapped children while riding a school bus. *Psychological Reports, 31,* 967–973.

Shehan, P. K. (1981). A comparison of mediation strategies in paired-associate learning for children with learning disabilities. *Journal of Music Therapy, 18,* 120–127.

Sheikh, A. A. (1983). *Imagery: Current theory, research, and application.* New York: Wiley.

Skinner, B. F. (1953). *Science and human behavior.* New York: MacMillan.

Sparks, R., Helm, N., & Albert, M. (1974). Aphasia rehabilitation resulting from melodic intonation therapy. *Cortex, 10,* 303–316.

Stein, J. K. (1973). Musicology for music therapists. *Journal of Music Therapy, 10,* 46–51.

Suzuki, S. (1981). *Nurtured by love: A new approach to education.* New York: Exposition.

Tyson, F. (1981). *Psychiatric music therapy: Origins and development.* New York: Creative Arts Rehabilitation Center.

Van den Daele, L. (1967). A music projective technique. *Journal of Projective Techniques, 31,* 47–57.

Wheeler, B. L. (1983). A psychotherapeutic classification of music therapy practices: A continuum of procedures. *Music Therapy Perspectives, 1*, 8–12.

Wilson, C. W., & Hopkins, B. L. (1973). The effects of contingent music on the intensity of noise in junior high home economics classes. *Journal of Applied Behavior Analysis, 6*, 269–275.

For Further Reading

Birkenshaw, L. (1994). *Music for fun, music for learning* (3rd ed.). St. Louis: MMB Music.

Bitcon, C. H. (1989). *Risk it-express! Expression in creative practice.* St. Louis: MMB Music.

Bonny, H. L., & Savary, L. M. (1973). *Music and your mind: Listening with a new consciousness.* New York: Harper & Row.

Boxill, E. H. (1989). *Music therapy for living: The principle of normalization embodied in music therapy.* St. Louis: MMB Music.

Bright, R. (1991). *Music in geriatric care: A second look.* Wahroonga, Australia: Music Therapy Enterprises.

Cassity, M. D., & Cassity, J. E. (1994). *Multimodal psychiatric music therapy for adults, adolescents, and children: A clinical manual.* St. Louis: MMB Music.

Clark, C. A., & Chadwick, D. M. (1980). *Clinically adapted instruments for the multiply handicapped.* St. Louis: Magnamusic-Baton.

Crain, C. D. (1981). *Movement and rhythmic activities for the mentally retarded.* Springfield, IL: Charles C. Thomas.

Douglass, D. (1981). *Accent on rhythm: Music activities for the aged* (3rd ed.). St. Louis: MMB Music.

Frazee, J., & Kreuter, K. (1987). *Discovering Orff: A curriculum for music teachers.* New York: Schott.

Gilbert, J. P., & Beal, M. R. (1982). *Music curriculum guidelines for moderately retarded adolescents.* Springfield, IL: Charles C. Thomas.

Graham, R. M. (1975). *Music for the exceptional child.* Reston, VA: MENC.

Graham, R. M., & Beer, A. S. (1980). *Teaching music to the exceptional child: A handbook for mainstreaming.* Englewood Cliffs, NJ: Prentice-Hall.

Hardesty, K.W. (1979). *Music for special education.* Morristown, NJ: Silver Burdett.

Jaques-Dalcroze, E. (1967). *Rhythm, music and education.* New York: Dalcroze School.

Jones, B., & Hawes, B. L. (1987). *Step it down.* Athens, GA: University of Georgia.

Karp, C. L., & Butler, T. L. (1996). *Activity book for treatment strategies for abused children: From victim to survivor.* London: Sage.

Kenny, C. (1982). *The mythic artery: The magic of music therapy.* Atascadero, CA: Ridgeview.

Krull, S. W. (1981). *Circle time activities for young children.* Concord, CA: Circle Time.

Elliot, B. (1982). *Guide to the selection of musical instruments with respect to physical ability and disability.* St. Louis: Magnamusic-Baton.

Nocera, S. D. (1972). *Reaching the special learner through music.* Morristown, NJ: Silver Burdett.

Plach, T. (1996). *The creative use of music in group therapy* (2nd ed.). Springfield, IL: Charles C. Thomas.

Reichard, C. L., & Blackburn, D. B. (1973). *Music based instruction for the exceptional child.* Denver: Love.

Richards, M. H. (1966). *Teaching music through songs, hand signing and inner hearing.* Palo Alto, CA: Fearon.

Reuer, B., & Crowe, B. (1995). *Best practice in music therapy: Utilizing group percussion strategies for promoting volunteerism in the well older adult.* San Diego: University Center on Aging.

Robbins, C., & Robbins, C. (1980). *Music for the hearing impaired*. St. Louis: Magnamusic-Baton.

Schulberg, C. (1986). *The music therapy sourcebook*. New York: Human Sciences Press.

Shaw, J. (1993). *The joy of music in maturity: Innovative programs for seniors*. St. Louis: MMB Music.

Shaw, J., & Manthey, C. (1996). *Musical bridges: Intergenerational music programs*. St. Louis: MMB Music.

Streeter, E. (1993). *Making music with the young child with special needs: A guide for parents*. Bristol, PA: Jessica Kingsley.

Summer, L. (1988). *Guided imagery and music in the institutional setting*. St. Louis: MMB Music.

Wheeler, B. L. (1983). A psychotherapeutic classification of music therapy practices. *Music Therapy Perspectives, 1,* 8–16.

Wheeler, L., & Raebeck, L. (1985). *Orff and Kodaly adapted for the elementary school*. Dubuque, Iowa: W.M.C. Brown.

O music
   In your depths we deposit our hearts and souls.
   Thou has taught us to see with our ears
   And hear with our hearts.

                        —*Kahlil Gibran (1883–1931)*

Chapter 9

The Music Therapy Treatment Plan

Occasionally, students or interns who observe my music therapy sessions comment on how spontaneous I appear. They question why I have asked them to prepare a formal treatment plan and a daily log for each session. Because I have no notes in front of me or because my attention is focused so directly on the person in therapy, they assume that I have not prepared the session and am acting completely on instinct. In fact, this is far from the truth. My preparation is so complete that my instruments and materials are within easy reach. My plan is memorized. I even have some contingency plans if the person does not respond to any one of the music experiences I have in mind. This frees me to be present in the therapeutic process and as attentive as I can be to this person with me.

This is one rationale for developing a detailed music therapy treatment plan. Another reason is that music therapy must be consistent with other treatments in meeting the person's needs. Whether working with an individual or group, the music therapist develops an individualized plan based on information gathered through the referral and assessment process. The plan begins with a hierarchy of objectives or responses outlining how the client is expected to progress throughout the therapy. Selection of an appropriate design structures the way in which therapeutic music activities are applied so that their effects can be measured.

A systematic plan is the outgrowth of work accomplished in the preliminary stages of music therapy. Evaluating the referral, assessment data and observational findings is an important start. Then, the therapist establishes a hierarchy of objectives which is either a developmental sequence of steps, a task analysis, or a chain of increasingly complex social responses. This list outlines the expected course of therapy. Next, the therapist determines whether individual needs can be met best in a group setting or individual therapy. The design of the music therapy program entails another major decision for the therapist. This chapter describes a few of the many clinically oriented designs, including *case studies* and a sampling of *experimental group* and *single subject designs*.

Beginning to Plan

Deryk, an eight-year-old student with a learning disorder, attends the third grade in his local public elementary school. He was referred to music therapy to improve the flexibility and fluidity of gross motor movements. Assessment activities included musically-accompanied tasks where Deryk was asked to imitate arm and leg movements, identify various body parts, and follow the therapist in moving around the room. Observations yielded the expected stiffness in gait and rigidity in posture. Most striking was Deryk's inability to imitate the therapist's motions, point to body parts, or follow simple instructions. Based on these data, the music therapy plan will focus on these very basic prerequisite skills before attacking the problem of flexibility.

A music therapy group at the Center for Speech-Delayed Children focuses on early language development. The objective for each group participant involves improvement in verbal expression of thought, leading to the use of complete sentences. The assessment device, a developmental checklist, shows that each child demonstrates a different level of receptive and expressive language func-

tioning. The therapist's challenge is to individualize treatment within the group setting.

In a psychiatric in-patient program, a group of clients meets with the music therapist in a series of songwriting sessions. Observation in other psychotherapy groups reveals that the clients are generally resistive to discussing their problems, and tend to deny the possibility that workable solutions exist. The music therapy group objective will be to create a musical composition based on ideas, experiences, and feelings of group participants. Each individual will be asked to consider present and past experiences, and to project desirable changes in each of their lives. Personal objectives and specific plans for future action will be incorporated in song.

In these examples, the music therapy plan is in various stages of formation. Collecting the evidence they have gathered, the therapists develop individualized plans to meet each of their clients' needs.

Assessing the Assessment

Now having the reason for referral, overall assessment and pretest or baseline observations, these data must be examined in light of response definitions and objectives which have been written already. Are these sources of information consistent with one another? Has the more detailed evaluation of behaviors by the music therapist resulted in a different perspective on the problem or target behavior?

It is advisable to review and revise the original response definition, if necessary, before proceeding. In Deryk's case, described above, assessment yielded vital information concerning lack of prerequisite skills for participation in an instructional program to improve flexibility.

Often, the very act of observation or recording will change a behavior such that it is no longer a problem. If I inform you that I intend to watch your nail-biting behavior, you may very well fail to do it in my presence. It is possible that having had your attention called to nail-biting, you will begin to restrain yourself when I am not present, as well. In this way, nail-biting decreases as a result of observation alone. When I take note of my own nail-biting behavior by recording its occurrences on a piece of paper, I usually find that my paper is blank at the end of the observation period. In fact, self-monitoring of behavior has been shown to be an effective behavior change strategy in certain instances (Kazdin, 1974).

Systematic observation may also indicate that the reason for referral does not reflect the most important target behavior for therapy. For example, assessment can illuminate the problem of inattentiveness in class as the result of a minor hearing loss, negating an assumption of motivational difficulty in the child. More obviously, a behavioral analysis may reveal that a problem of stealing does not belong to the one accused, but to those culprits who have set up the person for the crime. Thus, assessing the assessment will, frequently, require communicating with the source of the referral or the clinical team.

Response Hierarchies and Objectives

Now that short-term and long-term objectives have been established, there will be many steps or sub-objectives to be achieved along the way. While some objectives reflect a simple quantitative change, e.g., to increase social interaction (time spent with peers) from a baseline of zero to 30 minutes per day, or to eliminate acting out in the classroom, others call for a change in the nature of responding. The more qualitative difference may be delineated in a *hierarchy of objectives* or behaviors.

Developmental Sequence of Objectives

For the group of speech-delayed children described in this chapter, it is appropriate to construct a hierarchy of objectives denoting increasingly complex use of language rather than a mere increase in the number of words spoken. First, prerequisite skills must be specified. In this case, these skills are those necessary for successful participation in the group. Prerequisite skills also include psycho-social, physical and cognitive demands of the tasks being performed by the person, and generally refer to those assumptions that are made about the person's abilities before attempting a task. For the speech-delayed children, the following were prerequisites to group involvement:

1. Ability to sit in a chair for the duration of the session;
2. Elimination of major interfering social behavior;
3. Ability to attend to the therapist and/or task when appropriate, e.g., eye contact when called upon;
4. Ability to imitate basic responses, e.g., clapping, playing simple percussion instruments; and
5. Ability to follow a simple instruction, e.g., "Do this."

Clinical Example

In the area of language, developmental specialists and speech pathologists have determined that there is an order to the process of learning language. This list of basic to advanced language skills forms a hierarchy of expectations or objectives. The following is a very broad outline of such developmental objectives toward a terminal objective:

Terminal Objective
> Verbal expression of thought in complete simple sentences.

Verbal Receptive
1. Object identification ("Show me the drum.")
2. Performance of simple actions ("Ring the bell.")
3. Performance of actions involving spatial placement ("Put the drum on the chair.")

4. Following sequences of actions ("Stand up, clap your hands, then sit down.")
5. Pairing related objects ("What goes with the drum stick?")
6. Sorting similar objects ("Take the shiny instruments.")
7. Performance of actions involving body-space awareness ("Turn yourself around.")
8. Performance of actions involving object-space awareness ("Play the tambourine up high.")

Verbal Expressive

1. Vowel imitation ("Say 'ah'.")
2. Consonant imitation ("Say 'mm'.")
3. Word imitation ("Say bell.")
4. Basic expression and identification
   a naming simple objects ("What is this?")
   b. discriminating possession ("Who has the drum?")
   c. naming object's placement ("Where is the tambourine?")
   d. naming missing object ("What is gone from the set of instruments?")
5. Constructing complete sentences.
   a. using noun and verb ("The bell rings.")
   b. using noun, verb and modifier ("The children sing loudly.")
   c. using noun, verb, and prepositional phrase ("The drum is on the table.")
6. Using pronouns correctly ("I am Chuck. I have the maracas.")
7. Using correct tenses ("I played the wood block yesterday.")

While this sequence of expected language behaviors is generally simple to complex, a given child may respond appropriately at a "higher level" before being able to perform a "lower level" task, e.g., sorting objects before following a sequence of actions. Care must be taken to consider developmental objectives as general expectations. Do not make assumptions that because a child has only reached a certain level, achieving any more complex functions may not be possible. This is not intended to refute developmental theories on which these sorts of hierarchies are based. Rather it indicates that individual differences do exist, especially within the special education population.

Developmental Therapy

A developmental model has, in fact, been applied extensively in music therapy. Music has been established as a viable treatment modality within developmental therapy where ordered objectives are met through prescriptive music activities over four stages of growth: 1) responding to the environment with pleasure, 2) responding to the environment with success, 3) learning skills for successful group participation, and 4) investing in group processes. Objectives are also categorized by four curricular areas: behavior, communication, socialization, and academics. This approach is particularly useful with children who exhibit behavioral disorders and perceptual-motor difficulties (Purvis & Samet, 1976).

Task Analysis

Another type of hierarchy is a *task analysis*. This series simply orders objectives in the chronological sequence in which they would normally be performed. It also refers to steps of increasing difficulty such as might be required in a typical training program. The task analysis attempts to break down the task at hand or terminal behavior into the simplest step-by-step responses and order them logically. Here, the steps are listed as sub-objectives to the desired terminal short- and long-term objectives. The following is a task analysis of a therapeutic activity designed for Deryk:

Terminal Objective

To perform independent movements in sequence along with a recording of the song, "Head, Shoulders, Knees, and Toes."

Prerequisites

Motor ability to touch extremities.

Steps

1. Imitate model: Touch head with aid of physical and verbal prompts.
2. Same as step 1, with no physical guidance, but with verbal prompts and model.
3. Same as steps 1 and 2 with each of the following alone: shoulders, knees, and toes.
4. Imitate the two movements in sequence (head and shoulders) with model.
5. Imitate the two movements in sequence (knees and toes) with model.
6. Imitate entire sequence with model.
7. Imitate entire sequence with model as fast as recorded song.
8. Imitate entire sequence with song sung at a slow pace, using additional prompts and model.
9. Imitate entire sequence with song and model, no prompts.
10. Perform entire sequence with song and model of head, shoulders, and knees, only.
11. Perform entire sequence with song and model of head and shoulders only.
12. Perform entire sequence with song and model of head only.
13. Perform entire sequence with song and no model.
14. Perform entire sequence with recorded song at regular speed.

Social Hierarchies

Target behaviors which reflect learning a particular skill or developmental stage of growth may be complemented with an ordered set of objectives. In the area of social behavior, however, a hierarchy of expected responses may not be as clearly identifiable. Responses of increasing complexity may be difficult to define because they do not necessarily follow a specific temporal order. The hierarchy may be viewed as a continuum of desirable behaviors or objectives, with each delineating a successive approximation of the terminal objective.

The following is a hierarchy of objectives for the psychiatric in-patient group presented at the beginning of the chapter.

Response Definition

Contributions to songwriting group: Verbal statements, words, or phrases which can be incorporated into the song by the music therapist and are related to the topic or song theme. A single contribution is not greater than one line of song material.

Terminal Objective

To contribute a plan of action for the future and carry it out.

Hierarchy within Music Therapy

Contributing (as defined):

    1. a sung word or phrase;
    2. an idea to be expressed in song;
    3. a theme for the entire composition;
    4. an experience related to the theme;
    5. a feeling associated with the experience or theme;
    6. an alternative or plan for the future, related to the theme;
    7. a goal related to the theme;
    8. a personal objective toward the goal; or
    9. a series of objectives stated as a realistic plan of action.

Hierarchy for Generalization
1. Carrying out the first step of the plan in the music therapy setting (when applicable).
2. Carrying out subsequent steps in the music therapy setting.
3. Meeting the specified personal objective.
4. (Terminal Objective) Carrying out the plan and meeting the objective outside of music therapy.

Functions of Response Hierarchies

Whether it is a chronological, developmental, or increasingly complex sequence, the hierarchy of objectives serves several purposes. First, it functions as a behavioral checklist for assessing client progress. The highest level achieved in a given session or activity by an individual or group may be tabled or graphed, and compared with subsequent sessions to measure change. Alternatively, the number of times each objective is reached may be recorded on a bar graph or it may be weighted by level on the hierarchy and then graphed. Notice that in Figure 9.1, the contributions of John, Sally and Erin are graphed over four sessions. Both of these methods provide a way of evaluating progress on a continual basis. Secondly, the hierarchy provides a convenient outline for the music therapy plan. The therapist structures prescriptive music activities to meet each objective, thereby developing a program based directly on the person's needs. Thus, it is within the hierarchy framework that the therapist both plans and evaluates an individualized music therapy program.

Individual vs. Group Music Therapy

One of the decisions which the music therapist will make when devising a plan is whether to meet the client individually, within a group, or both. In many settings, the therapist will not be afforded the luxury of doing both group and individual sessions, or even of choosing between these options. But, given a choice, there are advantages to each.

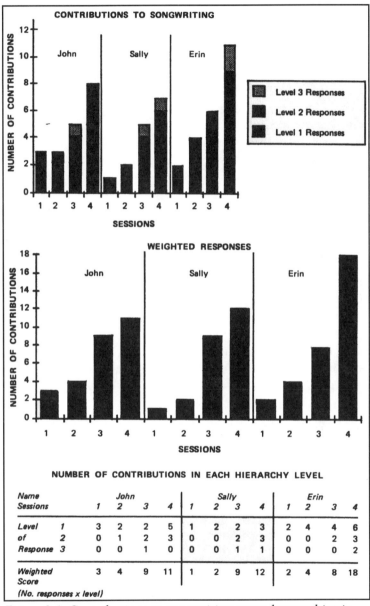

Figure 9.1. Contributions to songwriting group by psychiatric in-patients.

Individual therapy offers the one-to-one relationship and intensity of effort devoted to the person. It focuses on the precise functioning level of the person at any point in time. For the person who does not have the appropriate social behavior to participate in a group, it may also be the only acceptable alternative. Additionally, some analytically oriented or improvisation therapists will insist on individual therapy as the only viable means of treatment.

Group therapy is obviously a more cost-effective way of providing services, if it is appropriate and potentially successful. This factor aside, the use of group therapy techniques has been encouraged because of various therapeutic advantages. The social setting of the group may be a metaphor for interaction in the outside world, as has been discussed previously. But the group also provides an opportunity for each person to benefit from the support, empathy, helping strategies, and multiple perspectives of group members (Kaplan & Sadock, 1972). Additionally, in a more instructional type of program, group participants model appropriate responses and learn from one another in this way. The major challenge for the group therapist is to be able to individualize a program, taking into account each client's needs and functioning levels, and simultaneously attend to everyone.

Individualizing Group Music Therapy

The following are some basic guidelines for consolidating data gathered on individuals to form a group target and plan:

1. List target behaviors for each of the individuals.
2. Determine whether there are similar target behaviors or objectives common to two or more individuals. Then combine and re-label the class of other target behaviors which fall within this larger category of behaviors.
3. Determine whether it is possible to observe all of these behaviors simultaneously within the group setting. If not, it may be advisable to group people who share more similar targets.

4. Adapt response definitions and objectives, where necessary. Devise a group hierarchy and recording procedures.
5. Examine assessment data with regard to the ability of each person to function in a group or to meet prerequisite skills. Be particularly certain that elements such as instructional level can be geared to all persons in the group.
6. Devise music therapy assessment and treatment procedures which:
    a. allow each person to perform at an appropriate level,
    b. offer opportunities for the target behavior to occur and improve, and
    c. are well-suited for group participation.

Each of the speech-delayed children in the example described earlier exhibits unique language patterns and problems, providing just the sort of challenge of individualization referred to above. Four target behaviors emerge from the assessment given to group members:

1. Naming simple objects.
2. Use of complete sentences (with noun, verb, and object).
3. Discrimination of possession and placement.
4. Performance of actions involving object-space awareness.

The first three target behaviors involve expressive verbal skills; the last concerns receptive language. Observation reveals that two students in the group tend to act up when they are seated together or look at one another. All children are five or six years of age.

The music therapist must structure activities and employ consistent techniques of discipline to minimize disruption by the two students who display this tendency. Beyond that, each activity must offer opportunities to perform target behaviors. The group will learn simple, familiar children's songs such as

"Old MacDonald Had a Farm," "Mary Had a Little Lamb," and rhythmic chants based on the children's names. During each piece, the therapist will pause to ask certain children to name animals on the farm, characters in the song, children whose names are sung, or other song-related objects. Some will be asked to give complete sentences in their responses, or determine who is doing something in the song or group. Others will be required to hold up a specific picture, object or instrument and move it in a directed way. With a slight adaptation of popular children's games and songs, each of the target behaviors are dealt with in the group.

In a second group within the facility, the target behaviors are somewhat more diverse. The students are younger and not all of them demonstrate basic social skills necessary for learning in a group. The targeted areas include:

1. Performance of actions displaying
   body-space awareness;
2. Eye contact;
3. Ability to remain seated quietly for
   more than ten seconds at a time; and
4. Performance of simple actions
   upon instruction.

The therapist, aware of the variety of functioning levels, must provide active musical experiences which capture each child's attention while teaching basic receptive language. The activities must be rather tightly structured and carefully ordered to ensure that every child is capable of performing the required actions. With children who require remediation in such basic areas, the focus is on success-oriented experiences and enjoyable participation in games which facilitate learning. An example of such an activity is a simplified version of "Hokey Pokey," where the first sung command is "Look at me, (name of child)," and each verse ends with "Now, let's all sit down." With the therapist as model and the addition of physical guidance procedures when necessary, the children are led through various simple commands. Certain instructions which are appropriate for everyone can be given to the group; others should be individual commands. A single verse might be, "Sally, look at me, look at me, look at me. Everyone, do what I do, so watch and you'll see. Let's all stand up and turn around. Now, let's all sit down." This activity provides an opportunity to observe each of the target behaviors, and with the use of praise, physical and verbal prompting and modeling, can offer training in these areas as well.

With even more diverse targets, music therapists sometimes find it best to include one activity specifically designed to meet each of the target areas in a given session. Provided that every activity enables individuals to perform successfully at their own levels, participation which is not directly related to the clinical target may hold other benefits. Indeed, it may be inadvisable to focus entirely on an area in which a person is deficient. A session which offers participants an opportunity to display their strengths, experience success, and enhance their self-esteem while working on important problems or skills is a significant part of the music therapy process.

Design

By manipulating the conditions of music therapy over time, the music therapist is able to evaluate the person's progress as a function of music therapy. Adding a specific design to the treatment plan allows the therapist to gain as much information as possible about the impact of music therapy. This section presents the basic parameters of three types of designs: Case studies, experimental group designs and single subject designs. For more information on these and other ways to evaluate change, see Wheeler (1995).

Case Studies

In the clinical music therapy setting, a program may be structured in either of the following formats: 1) a *baseline-treatment* design comparing behaviors between these two conditions, or 2) a *pretest-posttest design* which compares results of testing before and after treatment. These are considered single case studies because they examine client progress in the case of one individual or group. The results of these studies are enlightening because they offer objective evidence of client change or lack thereof. However, there are limitations in the interpretation of these data. In the baseline-treatment design the therapist continues to collect the observational data gathered in baseline after the application of music therapy treatment. It is conceivable, however, that behavioral differences observed between baseline and treatment are attributable to factors other than music therapy. Suppose that a change in the client's home environment, use of medication, or other therapeutic programming occurs at the same time as the start of music treatment. Behavioral change could be the result of any of these variables.

The pretest-posttest design assesses functional levels before and after treatment. It is, likewise, subject to interpretive errors. Maturation, learning, or change in virtually any area could be responsible for pre- to posttest differences. Restraint must be exercised in assuming a cause and effect relationship between music therapy and behavioral change. In addition, caution is in order when drawing other conclusions based on these data.

How, then, may one gain greater certainty that music therapy is the critical component in the change process? The music therapy variable can be isolated with appropriate research designs, such as: 1) *experimental group designs*, or 2) *single subject applied behavior analysis designs*. These designs control factors which might contribute to change while testing the therapist's specific hypothesis.

Experimental Group Designs

Music therapists who work directly with several clients and have access to others can design a simple experiment to compare the effects of music therapy versus another type of treatment or lack of treatment.

Random Groups

Using one type of experimental group design, clients are randomly assigned to either an experimental group receiving music therapy, or a comparison/control group without music therapy. The therapist introduces specific music therapy techniques into one group, holding other variables constant. Such variables could be day of the week and place of treatment, length of session, or praise administered to clients. After the music therapy program is delivered, observations of behavioral change are taken, and comparisons are drawn between groups. This is an example of randomized subjects or *random group design*. With this attempt to control extraneous variables, the therapist has more assurance that post-treatment differences between group performance are attributable to music therapy, as in the following example.

The therapist at a community mental health center wishes to investigate the effect of an "imagery with background music" technique on relaxation of a group of patients. He randomly assigns the thirty patient volunteers who have been referred to therapy for anxiety reduction to an "imagery with music" experimental condition or a "background music only" comparison condition, with 15 clients attending each group. He decides to measure relaxation physiologically by observing heart rate, blood pressure, and galvanic skin response (GSR). The "imagery with music" group meets from 9 to 10 a.m. on Monday through Friday during a four-week period. Upon entering the room, the group hears tape-recorded instructions and then background music accompanied by a message to guide specific imagery experiences. At the beginning and end of the hour, the group is requested to remain in their places while staff members take pulse, blood pressure, and GSR recordings. The "background music only" group meets simultaneously in an adjoining room and hears the same announcements and background music, but does not receive the message suggesting specific images. The staff collecting physiological data rotate across the two groups so that a given staff member will record data of experimental group members one day and comparison group members the next. These staff are unaware of the experimental condition to which the clients belong. After two weeks, the groups exchange rooms to control location. The therapist, then, collates all data, and with the aid of statistical analysis, compares the relaxation results between groups.

This researcher is careful to hold extraneous variables constant by keeping the time frame the same and rotating both rooms and staff observers. Even the staff are "blind" as to experimental condition in order to limit this source of potential bias. Note that in this experiment, both groups receive intervention and volunteer to participate in the study. Such ethical safeguards are imperative when dealing with human beings, particularly in the investigation of therapeutic effects. In most facilities, a human rights or patient advocate council oversees such experimentation to ensure that the client's best interests are being served.

Correlated Groups

Another simple experimental group design involves the use of two or more "equivalent" or correlated groups of clients. Instead of randomly assigning clients to groups, the experimenter equates them on some relevant variable(s). Clients may be paired or matched on the basis of pretest performance or other factors which potentially influence the behavior of interest. They are subsequently assigned to different experimental groups. This is referred to as a *matched pairs design*. For instance, in an examination of a musical strategy to develop perceptual-motor skills in children with learning disorders, a vast range of motor performance was observed. The children were matched on their ability to perform certain perceptual-motor tasks, mental age, and school grade level, and then assigned to either a music or no-contact control condition. Generally speaking, it is preferable to randomize rather than match groups, but most important is that there is an equal chance that a client would be assigned to one group as another.

Another design "equalizes" control and experimental clients by having them serve as their own controls. Repeated observations of clients under different conditions is, often, a useful way of controlling variability which exists between groups prior to treatment. In this design, clients experience both control and experimental conditions as their performance under each is compared. This is also known as a *repeated measures design*. Thus, individuals might receive two forms of treatment, music therapy and non-music therapy based. At the completion of each treatment, changes in the target behavior are recorded. In order to control for treatment order, half of the clients might receive music therapy first, the other half experiencing non-music therapy based procedures first.

These experimental group designs enable the music therapist to build in ways of isolating music therapy as a major factor in behavioral change. With careful planning and structuring of sessions prior to the onset of treatment, it is possible to evaluate the effects of therapy scientifically.

Single Subject Designs

When it is inadvisable to work with large numbers of clients or to compare individuals receiving treatment other than music therapy, a different research design may be more appropriate. Further, group designs might not even elucidate an individual problem or its solution. When therapists are concerned with identifying the most effective strategy for a particular client, intensive, single-subject designs are more appropriate.

There are a number of single subject research designs employed by applied behavior analysts. Virtually all of them start with the collection of baseline data. Then, treatment is systematically applied at different points in time. The most common designs in music therapy research are the reversal and multiple baseline designs.

Reversal

The *reversal design* begins with the classic case study outline, baseline followed by treatment (see Figure 9.2). Next, in order to determine whether it is the therapy or some other factor that is responsible for behavioral change, treatment is withdrawn as baseline data are again recorded. Usually, for ethical purposes as well as those of experimental control, treatment is reinstated in a final phase. This results in an "A-B-A-B" design where "A" refers to the baseline and "B" to the treatment. Figure 9.2 is an example of eye contact in a multiply handicapped child who has four sessions of baseline, four of music therapy, four more sessions without music therapy, and the last four with music therapy again.

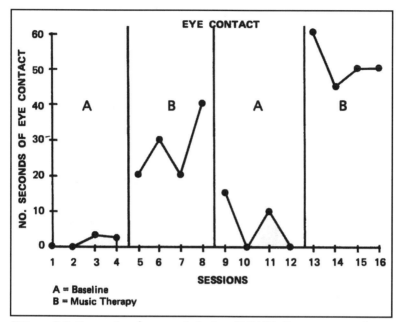

Figure 9.2. Example of reversal design (ABAB): Eye contact of multiply handicapped child.

Multiple Baseline

When it is not reasonable to "reverse" conditions in this way, a *multiple baseline* design may be more desirable. In Figure 9.3, Cheryl and Barry respond immediately to music therapy after both of them fail to respond at all during baseline. Here, baselines are simultaneously recorded either on a variety of target behaviors, on individuals, in different settings, or at various times of the day. After baseline appears to have been stabilized, treatment is applied to one behavior or element while baseline continues for the others. One at a time, the other elements are subjected to the same treatment. The multiple baseline offers a control over the time factor. For, it is highly unlikely that an effect which is replicated in several cases is due to a different variable presenting itself at precisely these points in time.

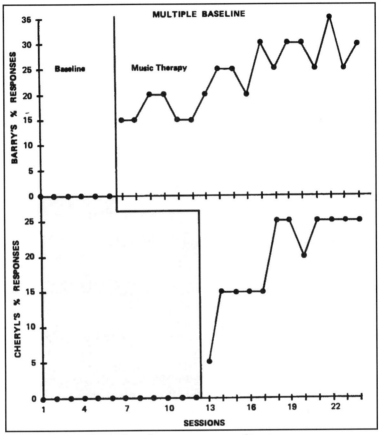

Figure 9.3. Multiple baseline across two clients.

The Formal Music Therapy Treatment Plan

With the selection of a set of music therapy strategies or protocol, the therapist formulates a formal proposal or plan for services. It is based on all of the evidence gathered to this point. The plan should be as specific as is feasible, offering options for adaptation of procedures when their actual impact is observed.

A written proposal of music therapy practices serves two functions: 1) it organizes the therapist's plan of action, and 2) it communicates elements of the program to others who are working with the person.

Standard clinical protocol calls for a statement of proposed procedures to be placed in a client's records. In accredited facilities, quality assurance procedures require assessment, treatment planning and evaluation. The formal Music Therapy Treatment Plan, designed for others to read and evaluate, is an important part of this process. Depending upon facility policy and therapist's needs, it may be lengthy and detailed, or a simple outline. It may reflect an individual's total programming, or introduce a group program to meet more general treatment goals. Examples and guidelines follow.

Individualized Treatment Proposal

The treatment plan or proposal is an outline of future programming over a designated period of time. This plan should both present a systematic program designed to meet treatment objectives and employ techniques which have the greatest probability of success. Because it is written primarily for the benefit of other professionals or those close to the client, it should use terminology which is understood by the prospective reader. It need not be extremely detailed, particularly since the therapist will wish to adapt procedures based on observations of responses to specific types of activities. However, this opportunity to communicate the music therapy program to others who are helping the person should result in a more informed network of team members, ultimately facilitating growth and change.

This individualized proposal should include procedures already employed in the initial and assessment stages of therapy in addition to proposed programming. Although the required degree of detail differs widely across therapists, the following outline is offered for its organization.

Music Therapy Proposal Guidelines

I. Client and Setting
   A. Client: Write a brief statement, giving age, gender, facility, reason for referral to agency and music therapy.

B. Setting: State frequency and duration of music therapy sessions, where they will take place, whether group or individual, and necessary materials/equipment.

II. Assessment Procedures
State target behavior(s) and response definition(s). Describe pretests and/or baseline observations. Summarize assessment findings.

III. Objectives
A. Goal: State the target behavior and direction of desired change for the goal. List short- and/or long-term goals, as appropriate.
B. Terminal Objective: State the terminal objective(s) of the hierarchy associated with goal(s) which are expected at the end of treatment.

Examples:

Goals	*Terminal Objective*
to improve manual dexterity	to play the "Hot Cross Buns" melody in tempo on the piano, using the correct three fingers on each hand; to type out words using letters in close proximity on a typewriter
to decrease acting out and learn	to accompany two songs in tempo by using two guitar chords, without disruptive behavior of talking or hitting (as specified in response definition)

C. Hierarchy of Objectives: List objectives in the order in which you expect them to occur.

IV. Treatment Procedures

    A. Antecedents: What will you do to prompt the target behavior, set the occasion for change, or teach a new skill? Will you specifically cue behavior by modeling, physically guiding or offering hints? What conditions will you set up to provide a stimulus for desired responses?

    B. Consequences: Will there be an immediate consequence for the target behavior? Will there be a consequence for other appropriate behaviors? What will occur when there is no response, an inappropriate response, or failure to improve?

    C. Techniques: Detail your approach to the problem, specifying the techniques you intend to employ, e.g., teaching methodology, non-directive mirroring or reflection of feeling, active listening, behavioral techniques, etc.

    D. Music Therapy Strategies: Describe how music will be employed. List musical objectives and outcomes. How does music interface with other techniques and non-musical objectives?

    E. Generalization Techniques: How will you ensure transfer?

V. Design

Identify the type of design you will use to evaluate progress.

Sample Individualized Music Therapy Proposal

Client and Setting

Client: Wendy is a frail three-year-old who is developmentally disabled. She attends the Delayed Development Program for Young Children. She was referred for music therapy because while unresponsive to most stimuli, she reacts to sounds and appears to be more active when background music is being played.

Setting: Wendy will attend two 20-minute music therapy sessions per week in a secluded area of her classroom. She will meet individually with the music therapist, who will provide a variety of simple percussion instruments, musical toys, cassette player and tapes as well as a collection of brightly decorated noisemakers. A padded chair which supports her body will be made available to assist the therapist in positioning her head.

Assessment Procedures

Target Behavior and Definition: Responsiveness to the environment, operationally defined as Wendy's response to hearing her own name. It is measured by three behaviors: smiling, vocalizing, and turning the head in the direction of the speaker.

Smiling is the upward movement of the outer edges of the mouth, which must move together and be a clearly observable change.

Vocalizing is any audible vowel or consonant sound by Wendy. Only voluntary sounds will be recorded. Sound of hiccoughing, burping, or crying will not qualify as vocalizations.

Turning the head is examined when the speaker is directly to the left or right of Wendy. Her head must turn in the direction of the sound by making any visible movement or jerk at least 30 degrees from pointing straight ahead. The head must remain at least 30 degrees in the correct direction for a minimum of two seconds to be counted. Before recording this behavior, the therapist will ensure that Wendy's head is facing straight ahead.

These behaviors are recorded only from the time the word "Wendy" is spoken until three seconds following its completion. Employing related event recording, the therapist records "Wendy" prompts and symbols representing smiling and vocalizing when any of these responses occur within the time allotment. Turning of the head is tested only when the therapist is positioned directly to one side of Wendy, and Wendy is facing straight ahead. The percentage of prompts which are met with responses is calculated.

Assessment Results

Baseline rates of the above responses to Wendy's name are shown in Figure 9.4. Baseline was recorded in the music therapy setting, but without the aid of music. The therapist would speak Wendy's name, once in front of her and once on each side of her. This offered three opportunities to observe smiling and vocalizing to the name, and two chances to observe head turning. This was repeated five times for a total of 15 trials for smiling and vocalizing, and 10 trials for head turning. Results show that Wendy failed to smile or vocalize to her name during any of the 15 trials on each of three days. She turned her head toward the source of the sound somewhat more frequently.

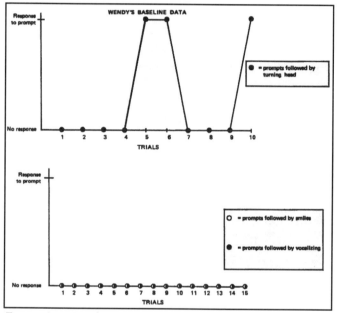

Figure 9.4. Baseline turning head, smiling and vocalizing for Wendy in response to hearing her name.

Objectives
To increase Wendy's rate of smiling, vocalizing and turning her head in response to hearing her name. This should occur at a consistent level both within the music therapy session and outside it when others call her name.

Treatment Procedures
Antecedents: A number of procedures will be used to set the occasion for smiling, vocalizing, and turning the head.

1. Experimentation with a variety of stimuli and observation of their effects. The music therapist will introduce feathers and objects of different textures, flashlights, music boxes and toys, percussion instruments, and brightly colored sound makers.
2. Rocking and stroking Wendy to background music while humming or singing along.

Consequences: When Wendy responds in any active or positive way, the therapist will praise her enthusiastically, pat, hold or hug her, and provide music and/or other stimuli to which she has demonstrated a positive response.

Techniques: The therapist will sing "Wendy" while presenting other sensory stimuli. Attempting to demand Wendy's attention, the therapist will vary the pitch and volume of the "Wendy" song. Using multiple combinations of stimuli and simple melodies for the "Wendy" prompts, the therapist will alternately cue and praise responses to the sung name. The therapist will physically guide the playing of percussion instruments while Wendy is swaying in the therapist's lap to background music. Throughout the session, the word "Wendy" will be sung or spoken repeatedly along with other simple statements, such as "I like you," "Play with me," and "Play some music."

Generalization Techniques
Just as in baseline, the therapist will test Wendy's response to hearing her name every four minutes by speaking it once in front of her and once on each side. In the twenty-minute session, this offers the same number of total trials as previously recorded. This will also test the generalization effects. After Wendy is responding consistently to the multiple stimuli during the treatment, the music will be phased out gradually until the therapist is merely calling her name. Other staff of the Center and Wendy's parents and siblings will be called into the session as often as possible to pair their words with the music and sensory stimulation. They will be encouraged to use Wendy's name during instruction and at play time at home and in other settings.

Design

To test the theory that Wendy will be more responsive to music, the following design will be employed:

Condition A. Baseline I. As described and shown in Figure 9.4.

Condition B. Music Prompts. During the next four sessions, the music therapist will test Wendy's responses to music as described in Generalization Techniques with the exception that her name will be sung and paired with music or sensory stimuli. The percentage of prompts met with defined responses will be graphed.

Condition C. Baseline II. An interval of three days will be arranged before the next music therapy session. During this time, three daily sessions will be held without music, resembling the Baseline I condition. Data will be recorded as they were in Baseline I.

Condition D. Music Prompts. This will replicate the Music Prompts Condition B and continue until a stable, high level of responding is maintained.

Condition E. Generalization Training. Music prompts and stimuli will be phased out very gradually as described. Responses to spoken name will be recorded, but music treatment will continue during the rest of the session. When Wendy is responding consistently to music and other stimuli, the therapist will begin to phase out these stimuli as well as the use of musical prompts.

Music Therapy Group Proposal

There is another type of treatment plan which generally requires less detail. In contrast to the therapist designing a completely individualized plan, often a music therapist organizes sessions for persons with similar needs. Individualization of treatment occurs within the session as the therapist observes and assesses each person. A group treatment proposal is necessarily less precise, and frequently functions as a set of guidelines for referring persons to the music therapy group. The following is an example of such a group proposal.

Introducing a Music Therapy Group for Oncology Patients

This group will meet twice a week for one and a half hours. It will be composed of eight to twelve oncology patients who have been diagnosed as having life-threatening illnesses such as cancer. The objectives of the group are:

1. to provide a supportive setting for patients with severe, chronic, or terminal illnesses;
2. to offer an environment where patients can express and discuss their feelings about their illnesses and present states;
3. to teach patients new ways to recognize and communicate these feelings; and
4. to help patients work out problems and adjust to limitations in an atmosphere of mutual assistance.

Music Therapy strategies will include:

1. composition of songs which express present feelings;
2. listening to and discussing music with themes related to problem-solving, optimism, looking at one's strengths, etc.;
3. learning new musical skills through participation in a small vocal ensemble with simple instrumental accompaniment (emphasizing each person's unique, creative talents and contributions to the group);
4. relaxation training through music listening with guided imagery;
5. nonverbal communication exercises which employ musical means of expressing ideas (while engendering awareness of their emotional components); and

6. projective problem-solving methods such as role-playing using one song which introduces the players and situation, and another song, composed by the group, to summarize the experience.

Evaluation of the group will be accomplished through a self-administered inventory, given pre- and post- each group session. Each patient will be asked to identify present feelings and psychological states by selecting appropriate adjectives from a list. An open-ended question will require a personal account of how each patient feels. The posttest will also include an open-ended question regarding any changes perceived by the patient.

Summary

The music therapy plan is set down before a formal treatment program is initiated. The plan includes a review of the assessments, a list or hierarchy of specific objectives, a brief description of the strategies, and a design. The hierarchy delineates: 1) developmental sequence, 2) task analysis, or 3) social hierarchy. It defines the steps through which client progress may be made. In the case of group music therapy, the next consideration is individualizing the plan. Guidelines are offered to assist the therapist in this process. The selection of design or basic structure of therapy is another important step. An appropriate design may help determine the effectiveness of music therapy. Although baseline-treatment and pretest-posttest designs are common, other designs are better able to isolate factors contributing to client change. Experimental group designs include random groups and correlated groups. Matched pairs and repeated measures are described as two types of correlated groups designs. Single subject designs include the reversal and multiple baseline. The music therapist may choose among these for the most feasible plan of action. With the addition of the music therapy strategy, the Music Therapy Treatment Plan is complete.

Key Words

Baseline-treatment design
> A design which compares behavior under conditions of no treatment and treatment of some kind.

Case studies
> Examinations of clients undergoing treatment, generally reporting the progress of a single case or group over time.

Experimental group design
> Any of a number of designs which employ scientific methods to test a hypothesis and control experimental variables in a highly structured manner.

Hierarchy of objectives
> A logical sequence of behavioral expectations leading toward the desired outcome of therapy.

Matched pairs design (correlated or equivalent groups)
> An experimental group design which first equates two groups of subjects on the basis of some relevant criteria; assigns one to a treatment condition and one to a condition without treatment; and then compares the performance of the two groups.

Multiple baseline design
> A single subject, applied behavior analysis design in which a treatment is added successively to two or more subjects, behaviors, settings or other similar units, while other conditions are held constant. The level of the target behavior(s) is observed throughout the baseline and treatment conditions.

Pretest-posttest design
> A design which samples behavior prior to and following treatment as an indication of progress or improvement.

Random group design (randomized subjects)
> An experimental group design which randomly assigns subjects to treatment conditions and compares performance of groups undergoing treatment vs. without treatment.

Repeated measures design
> An experimental group design in which repeated observation of subjects under different treatment or no treatment conditions allows subjects to act as their own controls.

Reversal design (ABAB design)
> A single subject, applied behavior analysis design which generally involves observing behavior during baseline, treatment, a return to baseline, and treatment reapplied.

Single subject, applied behavior analysis design
> A research design which assesses the effect of treatment. It refers to a group of "within-subject" or "intensive" designs which examine the behavior of one person or group over time.

Task analysis
> A detailed breakdown of the behaviors involved in a particular skill or task, listed in the order of occurrence.

References

Kaplan, H. I., & Sadock, B. J. (1972). *Models for group therapy*. New York: Dutton.

Kazdin, A. E. (1974). Self-monitoring and behavior change. In M. J. Mahoney, & C. E. Thoresen (Eds.), *Self-control: Power to the person*. Monterey: Brooks/Cole.

Purvis, J., & Samet, S. (1976). *Music in developmental therapy: A curriculum guide*. Baltimore, MD: University Park.

Wheeler, B. (1995). *Music therapy research: Quantitative and qualitative perspectives*. Phoenixville, PA: Barcelona Publishers.

For Further Reading

Baer, D. M., Wolf, M. M., & Risley, T. R. (1968). Some current dimensions of applied behavior analysis. *Journal of Applied Behavioral Analysis, 1,* 91–97.

Campbell, D. T., & Stanley, J. C. (1963). *Experimental and quasi-experimental designs for research.* Chicago: Rand McNally.

Hadsell, N. A. (1993). Levels of external structure in music therapy. *Music Therapy Perspectives, 11,* 61–65.

Madsen, C. K., & Madsen, C. H., Jr. (1970). *Experimental research in music.* Englewood Cliffs, NJ: Prentice-Hall.

Standley, J. (1991). *Music techniques in therapy, counseling and special education.* St. Louis: MMB Music Inc.

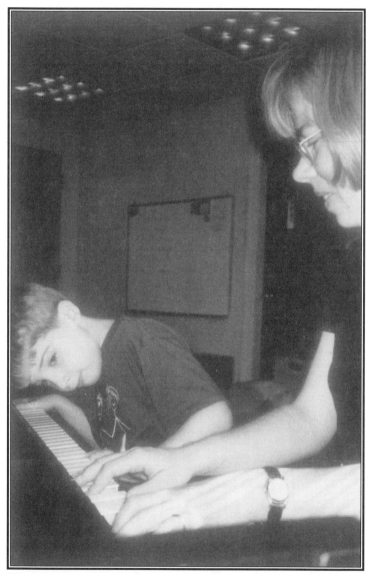

Music... can name the unnamable and communicate the unknowable.

—*Leonard Bernstein, 1976*

Chapter 10

Implementation

When I implement the music therapy treatment, all of my planning gives me the structure, format and preparation to move forward. With this foundation, I am free to imbed myself in therapeutic process and to engage fully in the therapeutic relationship. This chapter presents several ideas to facilitate the music therapy process as it is implemented. These include:

1. preparing a more complete contract delineating expectations and responsibilities of both therapist and client regarding treatment;
2. arranging a set of tables and/or graphs for recording target and other related behaviors;
3. constructing a daily log for music therapy session planning;
4. creating a form for recording session-by-session progress over the course of therapy;
5. consulting with colleagues and related professionals to devise a plan for clinical supervision;
6. reviewing the status of the therapeutic relationship; and
7. attending to changes in the course of music therapy and making appropriate revisions.

These considerations help the music therapist remain on track and accountable to the client. They also point out the importance of flexibility as the person's needs change over time. This chapter offers guidelines and examples to assist the therapist as music therapy is implemented.

Contracting

When therapy begins, the music therapist devises a preliminary contract. Now that the person's needs have been assessed and program planning is underway, the therapist can be more explicit in some of the areas only alluded to previously. The cooperation of the person and significant others is foremost in successful therapy. Ethically, it is important for the contract to specify a voluntary commitment on the person's part to participate in the program. Additions to the original contract should include a description of treatment procedures and also, conditions for the termination of therapy. The major reason for the termination of music therapy is usually the achievement of the therapeutic goal. However, the therapist may wish to include a trial period, at which time a formal evaluation of progress and accompanying recommendations would be presented. At that time, the person or responsible other would determine whether to continue music therapy for a pre-determined period of time. Follow-up procedures could also be outlined.

Depending upon the circumstances and nature of the referral, it is recommended that the contract stipulate as much as possible. Building upon the contract drafted at the first meeting, the therapist should reiterate or elucidate more about the working relationship, including:

1. logistical details i.e., frequency, duration, day, time and place of sessions, cancellation policy, attendance expectations;
2. ground rules e.g., fees and their collection, contingencies if therapist and client should meet outside of sessions, ethical considerations and confidentiality;
3. the reason for referral and the nature of therapeutic objectives;
4. brief description of music therapy approach, techniques or musical outcomes;

5. plan for review of progress, evaluation and follow-up; and
6. plan for termination.

A sample contract follows:

I, Susie Music Therapist, will implement a three-month, weekly music therapy program to assist Robert C. in learning basic academic skills through music. I will show Robert how to play two songs on the piano and improve his letter, number and word recognition. At the end of this period, the objective is to have Robert matching letters and numbers to notes on the keyboard and reading at least ten new words by sight. I will teach Robert from 3:00 to 3:30 p.m. every Wednesday at my studio. In the event of an unforeseen circumstance, I will make every effort to cancel the session at least 24 hours in advance, and reschedule during the same week. In three months, I will hold a conference with Robert's parents to discuss his progress and determine future objectives, at which time they will decide whether to continue music therapy.

I, Robert C., agree to practice the piano every day, even if it is for only a few minutes. I will keep a log of practice time, with my mother's help, and bring it to music therapy. I will complete the homework assignments given to me each week. At the session, I will pay attention and do my best to do everything the therapist asks. I will attend a half-hour session once a week. If I must cancel a session, my mother agrees to call at least 24 hours in advance, unless there is an emergency.

Tables and Graphs

Baseline and pretest data have already been recorded. Barring any changes in observation or testing procedures, these measures can continue to be plotted on the same figures. With successive phases of treatment or changes in design, it is important to remain consistent in data collection procedures and to label these segments of therapy accordingly. Reliability between observers continues to be an important factor in producing "believable" results, and so, should be checked and reported on a regular basis. Figures 10.1 and 10.2 illustrate two attempts to record progress as a function of music therapy.

Figure 10.1 is a graph of individual on-task behavior. The decrease in the rate of these behaviors during baseline means that treatment should begin soon. Note the reliability observer's data point on the graph. The discrepancy between these recordings reflects a 90% inter-observer reliability coefficient. Figure 10.2 is a table of spelling test results for a group of students. Pretest scores are listed for each student, with a mean calculated to serve as a basis for comparison with posttest results.

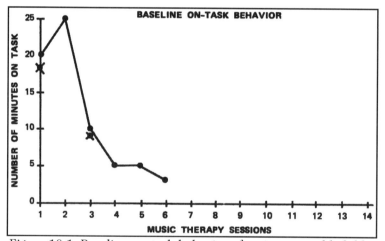

Figure 10.1. Baseline on-task behavior of a nine-year-old child.

PRETEST SPELLING SCORES	
Jamie	50
Tang	48
Gabriela	32
Ameeta	55
Van	69
Chue	30
Maria	36
Carlos	40
Tanisha	35
Kyle	55
$\overline{X}$ =	44

Figure 10.2. Pretest spelling scores for ten children.

Session Log

Just as a lesson plan is useful in structuring a classroom teacher's behavior, the music therapist's daily session log ensures that goal-oriented music experiences correspond with therapeutic objectives. The log resembles a lesson plan in that it identifies specific techniques, instruments, music or other materials, visual aids, and a step-by-step procedure. This should not prevent the therapist from being either spontaneous or flexible. The music experiences in a given session may depart from the original treatment plan as long as they are consistent with the established objectives. The therapist should, in fact, adapt and modify techniques, taking into account the needs of the person at each moment.

Here is a log for a group session with three young girls with pervasive developmental disorders, focusing on attention to the task and short-term memory:

OBJECTIVE: To have each child recall short sequences of activities which were performed in the session.

MATERIALS: Triangle, two drums, claves, tambourine and cymbals placed on table in front of room. Guitar will be used to accompany.

MUSIC: "When You're Happy and You Know It" (A visual aid with words or music is unnecessary as the children do not read, and the target behavior is attention to therapist or rhythm instrument.)

PROCEDURE:
1. Sing the familiar "Hello Song" to introduce Music Time.
2. Sing "When You're Happy and You Know It." Ask children to "sing along and do what I do." Incorporate clapping hands, stamping feet, tapping head and shouting "Hooray!" in four verses.

3. Ask each child individually to recall the name
of the song and "one thing we did" while
singing. Record responses, then prompt and
praise as necessary.
4. "Next, we are going to play instruments while
we sing. Who remembers the name of this instrument?" Hold up each of the six instruments. Then,
test the children individually to determine the
number of instruments identified correctly. After
the first correct response, allow the child to take
that instrument and place it on the floor.
5. Sing "When You're Happy and You Know It, Play
the_____," requesting the children to play
only when their instrument is called.
6. Take the drum and sing to the tune of "Looby Loo":
I have an instrument.
One I can play all day.
If you have the_____,
Stand up and play what I play.

Have children imitate one, then two and three drum beats.
If all three are mastered, play softly, loudly and a combination of soft and loud beats promptly and precisely. Then test
each child, recording the highest level of accomplishment.
7. Ask children to find the_____(a different
instrument), trade instruments, and sing song again.
8. Ask children to name the two instruments they just
played.
9. Chant:
Watch and do.
Watch and do.
I'll do something
Then you do it, too.

Ask children to imitate simple movements, one by one,
then in a series. Introduce by saying, "Watch." (Do movement.) "Do." (Assist children to do movement.) Repeat
movements and assist until group can imitate relatively
independently and wait for the cue, "Do."

10. Ask children to demonstrate one of these move-
    ments as they take turns leading the group while
    the therapist instructs, "Watch" and "Do."
11. Sing "When You're Happy and You Know It, Do
    This," as children take turns leading the group in
    movements.
12. Ask each child to recall one movement performed
    in the song by saying "Show me one thing we did in
    the song." Model one, if necessary. Prompt, praise
    and record appropriate responses.
13 Sing, to the tune of "Looby Loo":
    Let's put away the_____(instrument)
    Let's put away the_____(instrument)
    _____(name) will you get the
    _____(instrument)
    And put it away in the box.

Allow each child a chance to find an instrument and put it
away.

14. After each of four instruments are put away, ask
    children "Which instrument did we put away?"
    Continue with song, putting away last two instru-
    ments and asking "Which two instruments did we
    just put away?"
15. Sing the familiar "Good-bye Song," asking each
    child to name a song or activity which we did in the
    session.

Notice how this session log of music experiences incorporates
testing as well as training procedures, and individual as well as
group responses. Each activity is designed with the objective of
improving short-term memory by gradually increasing the level
of difficulty of a variety of musical tasks.

Progress Notes

Most facilities have adopted a standardized format for recording
client progress. Regardless of its specific configuration, each
progress note will include information on the target behavior

and other observations relevant to therapeutic progress for the permanent record. An ongoing assessment offers objective evidence of change in the target behavior, session by session. But, coupled with this should be a more informal, anecdotal analysis of each session. Most importantly, any change which could be of interest to staff, a sign of potential change, or an unusual occurrence should be noted in the chart or file. Incidents of any type must be reported immediately.

Often, responses or events observed during the session become potential target behaviors. For instance, Melanie was referred to music therapy as an adjunct to a speech therapy program to help her overcome stuttering and other articulation problems. While teaching her a variety of children's songs and some simple melodies on the recorder, it was observed that Melanie appeared happier and more self-confident as therapy progressed. The therapist started collecting data on smiles and positive statements during the session and also at recess time in the school yard. Comments from the classroom teacher supported observed positive changes in these secondary measures. Although there was no experimental control to determine the degree to which music therapy alone was responsible for these results, it became clear that the dramatic improvement in Melanie's self-esteem was a significant change in her life.

George, on the other hand, was responding sporadically to his music therapy program. Examination of the data revealed that the target behavior, participation in group activities, was great during motor activities such as marching and clapping, but very low during singing. Procedures were subsequently modified to require echoing one word, then imitating familiar words, and later, introducing sung phrases.

Patricia, a child with multiple physical and mental challenges, was making steady progress in music therapy. On certain occasions, however, Patricia displayed considerable lapses in concentration. Sharing anecdotal notes on these attentional problems with staff of the Rehabilitation Center, the music therapist learned that a new medication was being administered to Patricia which may have elicited these side effects. The music therapist's data were helpful in tracking the effects of the drug and ultimately, identifying a more reasonable dosage.

Progress Note Format

The writing of progress notes is somewhat of an art itself. Notes should be brief, specific, and objective. Generally, they are based on observed data and offer a succinct statement of progress or changes in behavior. Any outstanding or unusual events or changes are, of course, to be recorded as well. It is advisable for the music therapist to write progress notes on each client after each session.

The following are two examples of popular formats for keeping progress notes, known as APIE and SOAP notes. APIE refers to:

A for Assessment, observations of how the person presented in therapy

P for Plan, the goals and objectives which were the focus of the session

I for Intervention, techniques and strategies used by the therapist

E for Evaluation, progress in meeting goals and objectives

SOAP is a format developed prior to the APIE system. It is still used by many health facilities. SOAP refers to:

S for Subjective, a clinical impression of the person's presentation

O for Objective, the present condition as observed or measured

A for Assessment, observations of progress in the session

P for Plan, the goals and objectives

Sample Progress Note

Juan is in the middle stage of dementia and lives at home with his wife. The music therapist's goal is to decrease agitation and maintain a calm, attentive state. The therapist wrote this progress note after one group session:

A: Juan presented with confusion and disorientation. He repeated "But, I..., But, I..." at least ten times before starting to cry.

P: The session included singing songs and dancing to familiar music. The plan for Juan was to have him engage actively by singing a solo and dancing with a partner. These activities were selected to attract his attention and engage his active participation.

I: The therapist started the session with Juan's favorite song, the Brazilian "Casa Forte." He was asked to sing the verse solo and the group sang the chorus. He chose a dance partner, turning to Maria, and they danced together for the remainder of the session.

E: As soon as he heard "Casa Forte," Juan stopped crying and began to sing. He took the microphone willingly with a smile on his face. He sat calmly and focused his eye contact upon the therapist while the group sang. He recalled the waltz steps and danced competently with Maria while continuing to smile. He left the session, exiting with the other participants at a relaxed pace. He said "Good-bye" to the therapist. There were no visible signs of agitation from the time that Juan began singing. He appeared content throughout the singing and dancing.

Clinical Supervision

When music therapists speak of their own clinical practices, they are playing multiple roles beyond being service providers. "Practice" refers to the therapy they provide, the relationships they build with clients, and the ongoing development of their own musical skills. Music therapists grow and learn as persons, clinicians, and musicians as they gain more experience. In their desire to refine, update and learn new skills, they may seek out expertise through consultation with experts, peers and related professionals.

This group of colleagues serves not only as a cadre of mentors or teachers, but also as a source of reflection for the music therapist to pose questions regarding therapeutic process and relationship. When a therapist seeks out a professional or group for the purpose of supervision, this collaboration may be formalized to meet the standards established by certain clinical facilities or governing bodies. Currently, clinical supervision is not required for a Board

Certified Music Therapist, but it may be mandated for providers of medically reimbursable services. Supervision is advisable for every therapist who is actively engaged in clinical practice.

Supervision may take many forms. It can be administered in groups or individually. The time may be used to review video or audio tapes of sessions. It may involve receiving guidance and counsel on handling particular cases or hearing an outside perspective on what is happening within the therapeutic encounter. More specifically, supervision may entail:

1. mentoring and teaching specific skills and competencies;
2. reviewing cases;
3. supporting a peer through challenging clinical experiences;
4. observing or monitoring music therapy sessions;
5. serving as the therapist's therapist to process issues which arise during music therapy sessions; and
6. providing a source of clinical judgment to assist in decision-making.

In several communities, music therapists gather informally to support each other and offer training on topics of interest. Other music therapists meet regularly with peers to provide ongoing feedback. Another model applies small group supervision with a psychologist, psychiatrist, or related professional. As music therapists become more accountable to their employers and their constituents, they are being called upon to demonstrate their commitment to improving the quality of their work through obtaining clinical supervision.

The Evolving Therapeutic Relationship

The therapeutic relationship is considered by many to be the most influential factor determining success in therapy. It is definitely instrumental in affecting change, and it is dynamic. As every relationship does, it evolves over time with an ebb and flow that should be monitored carefully. The relationship between music therapist and client is enhanced by their relationships to the music. The music therapist uses music to bridge the interpersonal relationship further, adding richness and depth to this shared experience.

There are many dimensions to the therapeutic alliance. Brammer and Shostrom (1968) cite several factors. Uniqueness and commonality refer to the ways in which people are different and the same. Music therapy emphasizes the unique musical expression of every individual while enabling people to engage interactively in a common experience. The relative amount of intellectual and emotional content in the relationship constitutes a second set of factors. Music therapy requires varying degrees of analytical competence, while providing opportunities to feel emotions at a peak level. Ambiguity and clarity form a third dimension. In the music therapy context, music provides a clear direction when the person plays or sings on cue. Yet, there can be intense ambiguity when a group is improvising freely. The last dimension, trust and distrust, is built into every relationship. Within success-oriented music therapy, rapport and trust tend to come easily. Thus, engaging the person through music opens the way for great depth of experience along these continua. The therapist must be particularly vigilant to use the relationship productively and sensitively to help the person in therapy.

Within psychoanalytic approaches to music therapy, two concepts are central to therapeutic process. *Transference* is the way in which the client projects relationships with key figures in life directly to the therapist. *Countertransference* refers to the therapist's projection of feelings and behaviors toward others onto the client. Working with and through transference and countertransference is a significant part of psychoanalytic music therapy. In other approaches, the interpretation of the relationship may not be as extensive, but an analysis of empathy and *phenomenological* experiences with persons in therapy is every bit as important. Empathy is the sense of understanding another person's feelings, thinking and actions such that there is a sense of accompanying the person directly in the process. Phenomenological experience refers to the perception of subjective reality, as opposed to physical and objective description. Several music therapists have devoted great effort to describing private reactions to the person (Lee, 1996; Wheeler, 1999). Others have examined the personal meaning that comes with empathy (Amir, 1996; Bruscia, 1995).

Attention to the therapeutic relationship means that the therapist's and the client's independent and mutual processes are being monitored and examined. It is useful to share observations and perceptions about the relationship in clinical supervision. The outside observer lends an objectivity to this subjective analysis.

Revision of Procedures

It is the rare case that everything proceeds according to plan without any deviation whatsoever. In fact, it is expected that the therapist will take cues from the person in varying the direction or emphasis of music therapy. Indeed, the person's responses at the moment guide the subtleties of therapeutic process. This must be accounted for within the treatment plan. With objectives leading the way, the therapist must adapt and detail the plan according to the changing needs of the client. Critically evaluating each session regarding its impact, the therapist must constantly renegotiate the best course of action based on ongoing observations and personal impressions. Therapists should trust clinical judgment in making decisions regarding whether or not a new response definition or target behavior is indicated. Although it may appear counter-productive, this cyclical process of reviewing earlier stages of the model yields greater knowledge about the person as a whole and is a crucial part of therapy. The music therapist must remain aware of the person's changing state and possible implications for therapeutic planning. Particular attention should be paid to:

1. new issues or behaviors which surface;
2. new directions in therapy which appear more congruent with the person's needs at a particular stage of therapy;
3. the need to consider new objectives; and
4. new strategies to meet changing needs.

Summary

This chapter covers several ongoing considerations as music therapy is implemented. They include contracting, tabling and graphing, session planning, describing client progress, obtaining clinical supervision, reviewing the therapeutic relationship, and revising procedures. These steps assist the therapist in determining the functional relationship between therapy and its effects. With constant vigilance, the therapist attends to changing client needs and makes any required changes in treatment plan. Clinical examples offer a glimpse of the decision-making processes undertaken by the therapist as music therapy progresses.

Key Words

Countertransference
    The therapist's projection of feelings, ideas and
    desires about others onto the client.
Phenomenological
    Perceived through subjective reality, as opposed to
    physically and objectively.
Transference
    The client's projection of feelings, ideas and desires
    about others onto the therapist.

References

Amir, D. (1996). Experiencing music therapy:
    Meaningful moments in the music therapy process.
    In M. Langenberg, K. Aigen, & J. Frommer (Eds.),
    *Qualitative music therapy research: Beginning
    dialogues*. Gilsum, NH: Barcelona.
Bruscia (1995). Modes of consciousness in guided
    imagery and music (GIM): A therapist's experience of
    the guiding process. In C. B. Kenny (Ed.), *Listening,
    playing, creating: Essays on the power of sound*.
    Albany, NY: State University of New York Press.
Brammer, L., & Shostrom, E. (1968). *Therapeutic
    psychology*. Englewood Cliffs, NJ: Prentice-Hall.

Lee, C. (1996). *Music at the edge: The music therapy experiences of a musician with AIDS*. London: Routledge.

Wheeler, B. L. (1999). Experiencing pleasure in working with severely disabled children. *Journal of Music Therapy, 36,* 56–80.

For Further Reading

Diaz de Chumaceiro, C. L. (1992). Transference-countertransference in psychology integrations for music therapy in the 1970s and 1980s. *Journal of Music Therapy, 29,* 217–235.

Knoll, C. D., Henry, D., & Anderson, S. E. (1999). *Music works: A professional notebook for music therapists*. (3rd ed.). Stephenville, TX: Music Works.

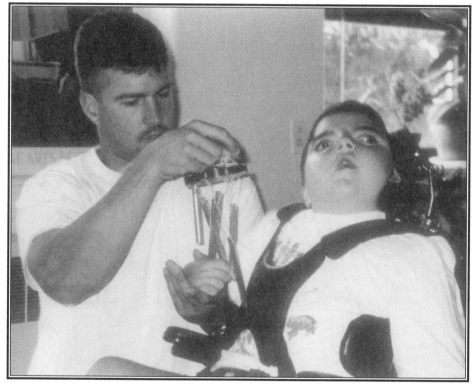

Bells are music's laughter.

—*Thomas Hood, 1827*

Evaluation

I am continually saying that my work as a music therapist allows me to exercise both sides of my brain. I am a musician and a scientist. I am subjective and objective about my work. I am deeply involved in the process while engaged in the therapeutic relationship and I am detached when I examine this process to evaluate the outcomes of music therapy.

This chapter is about stepping back from the therapy and evaluating with both ears and eyes. It is about looking at the data and interpreting what therapy has meant to the person. Quantitative and qualitative analyses paint a multi-colored picture.

Defining Success

The final evaluation of a music therapy program attempts to answer one major question: Was music therapy successful in meeting the established goal? The data-based model demonstrates the answer in a scientific manner through presentation of graphs and tables of behavioral results. These data may elicit more questions, however, about the nature of observed changes. For one, is progress directly attributed to music therapy? If therapists have built in an experimental or applied behavior analysis design, they may be able to address this question with confidence. Are behavioral changes evident to others evaluating the program? Has progress been made in various aspects of the person's life? These tangential concerns are certainly relevant to the "success" of therapy, and should be discussed in addition to objective results.

The failure to demonstrate improvement through therapy raises many queries. Did the therapist modify the program when changes in behavior were not forthcoming? What problems were encountered and how did the therapist attempt to rectify them? What other factors may have contributed to results? Both objective and less formal anecdotal data, gathered throughout therapy, may provide hypotheses to explain progress or lack of improvement.

Program evaluation usually employs assessments of the whole person or program, albeit in a less detailed manner than for a single target behavior. Open-ended tools allow the evaluator to address a number of general areas. Qualitative measures require different perspectives regarding success. Questionnaires and interviews are two popular, qualitative evaluation devices for polling the person and significant others. For individuals who are capable, self-evaluation is another valuable source of information.

Existing data files from schools, facilities and service agencies may provide evidence of program effectiveness and generalization. Information from IEPs, IPPs, and other client records indicate the status of related behaviors which may show progress in broader areas of functioning. Caution must be exercised to ensure that the myriad of factors responsible for changing a person's life are taken into account when drawing conclusions about the impact of music therapy alone. Because music therapy is often one of a team of services, it is as important to examine the effects of a total treatment approach as it is to isolate the influence of music therapy.

Secondary Gains

Behaviors related and unrelated to target behaviors are bound to change over the treatment period. In the music therapy literature, positive "side effects" are almost always reported, due to the many influences of music. These are known as *secondary gains* or outcomes. Increased pride in self, motivation to try new things, and enhanced fine motor coordination are some accompaniments to musical experience which are observed frequently. Although these results may not have been collected with as much rigor as target behavior data, it is important that they are recognized, documented, and communicated. Ideally, upon the first glimpse of changes in secondary areas, the music therapist has implemented a new data-gathering system for its accounting.

Recommendations For Future Action

The evaluation of treatment will also include recommendations for the future, including whether music therapy should be continued or terminated. New target behaviors and objectives may be identified in either case. An example of a proposed music therapy program to meet these needs could be in the form of a contract for continuation of services. If music therapy is to be terminated, follow-up procedures should be described in an attempt to ensure maintenance of the achieved gains.

Music therapy is a unique service in that there is always a higher level of creativity or musical achievement which is possible. In music therapy, a shift in focus to more advanced musical accomplishments can bring associated non-musical changes. Individuals who respond to music therapy can discover more of their potential through continued music training or therapy programs. For this reason, recommendations often include long-term involvement to maximize benefits and generalize musical outcomes.

Communication of Therapy Outcomes

Results of the music therapy program may be of interest to professional and paraprofessional staff, the person's significant others, administrative personnel and colleagues. A well-written and thoughtfully conceived program evaluation is of considerable value to those concerned with the person as well as therapists who work with similar referrals. Every new case teaches a lesson regarding the ways in which music can be employed therapeutically. Dissemination and communication of outcomes either through publication or oral presentation is a responsibility of the music therapist before the file is considered complete.

The language of such communication must be carefully considered. Professional jargon is acceptable when the audience is accustomed to hearing and using such verbiage. Reports to the person and family members should be devoid of technical terms while emphasizing the areas of progress which are of greatest concern.

Sample Music Therapy Evaluations

The following exemplify some of the multifaceted elements which may comprise a music therapy evaluation.

A Music Therapy Program to Reduce Everyday Stress

Clientele:
A group of 20 business people employed at a large bank participated. The bank contracted with the music therapist to provide music-facilitated relaxation training and music therapy for their employees.

Setting:
A large lounge area in the basement of the bank was set up with a stereo system to accommodate the program. The group met three times per week from 4:15 to 5:00 p.m. Sessions ran for a period of three months, when employees could elect to continue music therapy, advance to a different music therapy group, or discontinue the program.

Objectives:
1. To provide an opportunity to relax and prepare for the transition from work to home;
2. To teach relaxation techniques which participants may use whenever they are under stress;
3. To have people participate in an exercise program designed to recognize and relieve body tension while also increasing circulation to inactive areas of the body; and

4. To assist participants in developing a repertoire of music selections which may help them to relax at home.

Assessment Procedures:

Target Behavior: Body tension.

Response Definition: Body tension was measured by three indicators; blood pressure, pulse rate, and a self-check of tension in several parts of the body.

Pulse rate was taken by the therapist when participants first entered and when they left the room. Blood pressure was measured with a blood pressure cuff applied by the therapist after measuring pulse.

At the first session, participants completed a questionnaire regarding their favorite music. They were instructed in ways to recognize body tension. The therapist gave individual feedback while they determined whether they felt tension in any part of their bodies. When the group was ready to begin subsequent sessions, participants were instructed to move and manipulate isolated parts of the body to check for tension. Each person recorded notable tension with a check mark on individual data sheets which included blood pressure and pulse.

Tension in the face, neck, shoulders, back, abdomen, fingers, hands, arms, toes, feet and legs were checked by each person. The therapist assisted by checking two areas of the body in each person per session. This served as a reliability check while instructing participants in how to identify tension. At the close of each session, this procedure was repeated, yielding pretest and posttest body tension per session.

Music Therapy Procedures:

1. Each session began with individual physiological measurements, and self-checks of body tension. The therapist offered individual assistance and instruction in identifying such tension.

2. An exercise program, working each part of the body, was accompanied by rhythmic music representing a variety of styles, guided by questionnaire responses. Each of the

identified areas of the body was moved, first slowly, then more actively. Gradually, more aerobic movements were added until an integrated set of dance movements took place. Modifications of the movements made it possible for everyone to participate at a comfortable level.

3. The movements gradually slowed as the tempo of background selections decreased. All participants would finally be seated or lying down in preparation for relaxation exercises.

4. Systematic relaxation of the body was attempted through tensing and relaxing each area, one by one. Slow, rhythmic, instrumental music served as a background for this component of the program.

5. The music therapist gave specific suggestions to the participants regarding pleasant visual images as the music continued for approximately 15 minutes. Next, the therapist suggested that the group prepare for the evening by thinking of things that they wished to spend their time doing, ways that they could relax at home, or the possibility of setting aside some special time for enjoyment or relaxation. Time was provided for participants to imagine themselves in this positive environment and search for the details of the setting so that they could reproduce it later. In other sessions, participants visualized anxiety-producing situations in their lives while relaxing to the music.

6. The therapist prepared the group to return to the here and now. They discussed the images which they experienced and plans for the evening ahead. They discussed how the music affected them. Common elements across the more relaxing pieces were identified to enable participants to recognize them in other music. A homework assignment to identify relaxing music from their own collections was given.

7. A favorite selection, by group consensus, was played while a slow, flowing set of movements was performed. The group, then, performed self-checks of body tension, and as they left the room, physiological measurements were taken once again.

Evaluation: As 53 persons had originally registered for the music therapy program, 20 were randomly selected to participate, and the remaining 33 were placed on a waiting list. This enabled the therapist to compare the two groups in a Random Group Experimental Design. With the addition of such a comparison group, it was possible to develop an effective evaluative tool. Unfortunately, it was not feasible to take the same physiological measures in the group of non-participants. However, a broad questionnaire designed to examine the impact of the entire three-month program was administered easily to all 53 people.

The questionnaire consisted of a rating scale (1-5) in which the occurrence of the following events was estimated by respondents:

1. Always	2. Most of the time	3. Sometimes	4. Not Usually	5. Never

1. I feel relaxed_____.
2. There is some tension that stays with me_____.
3. I find it hard to change gears when I leave work _____.
4. I can relax when I need to _____.
5. I drink or smoke _____.
6. When under stress, there is tension in my body _____.
7. I take medication to help me relax_____.
8. Stress is a problem_____.
9. I use relaxation techniques_____.
10. My body is free of tension_____.

At the end of three months, participants were asked to comment on their personal experiences in music therapy.

Results:

Physiological Measures, Pre vs. Post: There were no significant differences between pre- and post- measures of either pulse or blood pressure. There was, however, significantly less body tension reported by the participants at the end of the music therapy session than at the beginning ($p < .05$) (see Figure 11.1). Interestingly, pre-session body tension generally increased during the second month, and decreased during the last month. Although this may have been due to increased pressures during the second month, it is also plausible that participants became more adept at recognizing tension. Since this was a self-report measure, there was no way of determining the reliability of these data. However, the purpose of the music therapy program was to have the employees themselves become aware of body tension and reduce it. Based on these data, this objective may very well have been accomplished.

MEAN BODY TENSION SCORE*		
	Pre-session	**Post-session**
Month 1	6.8	4.2
Month 2	7.5	4.0
Month 3	6.2	3.6
Mean for Program	6.8	3.9

* Body tension was scored by adding the number of areas of the body which were checked by each participant. A mean score was then calculated for the group of 20 participants.

Figure 11.1. Mean body tension scores of music therapy participants pre- post-sessions.

Questionnaire Responses, Participants vs. Non-Participants: Of the 33 non-participants, 25 completed the questionnaire. Of the 20 participants, only 16 who attended at least nine sessions were included in questionnaire data analysis.

Questionnaire responses of participants and non-participants at the beginning of the program were compared. A similarity in means and standard deviations and lack of any significant differences between the scores of the two groups supported the randomness of the selection process. At the end of the three month program, questionnaire responses of participants differed significantly from those of non-participants. Participants in music therapy also scored significantly more positively at the end of the treatment period than they had at the beginning (see Figure 11.2).

A majority of the participants chose to continue in music therapy programs, and reported success in using the techniques in stressful situations. In the open-ended final questionnaire, employees also stated that they looked forward to the sessions, learned a great deal, and enjoyed the training.

In the future, it would be of interest to determine whether participants in such a music therapy program have greater productivity on the job, remain employed at the bank longer, or enjoy better mental or physical health. The results of this program demonstrate impact in the areas to which it was addressed. More far-reaching questions may now begin to be explored.

MEAN QUESTIONNAIRE SCORES*		
	Pre-music therapy	Post-music therapy (3 months later)
Participants	28.5	33.3
Non-participants	28.0	28.2

*The higher the score, the more positive the response. Each rating on a single question was converted so that 5 was the most positive answer and 1, the most negative. Each person received a composite score by adding these ratings. The highest possible score was 50, the lowest possible was 10. The means of the entire group are given here.

Figure 11.2. Mean questionnaire scores, pre- and post-three-month period.

A Music Therapy Program for a Child with a Behavioral Disorder

Client and Setting:
Client: Alan is a 12-year-old boy who attends a special education class for children with behavioral disorders. Alan could not function well in the regular classroom because he often had unprovoked and uncontrollable outbursts or crying or yelling in the midst of a lesson. Said to have a low frustration tolerance, Alan would refuse to complete academic tasks in which he had any question about his competence. When he was at all unsure that he could answer a question 100% correctly, he might toss the paper away and begin to cry before attempting it. He was placed

in this self-contained classroom because of the emotional way in which he handled these situations. Alan showed little interest in any particular academic area, but when students were asked to volunteer for a guitar program, Alan responded enthusiastically.

Setting: For a period of six months, Alan worked with the music therapist who was employed at his school. Alan and three other students met once a week for a half-hour guitar lesson in the therapist's office. Alan borrowed a guitar belonging to the school during lessons and practice times.

Objectives:

Alan exhibited the same inability to follow through with a task during the initial guitar lesson. While very interested and anxious to play the guitar, he responded to instructions by saying "I can't" or "I won't," and refusing to attempt even the simplest task. Based on these observations and the teacher's reports of classroom behavior, the following music therapy objectives were established:

1. To decrease the number of refusals to either comply with instructions or attempt a response in music therapy, and
2. To increase the amount of time spent attempting to play or actually playing the guitar, as per instructions.

Outside of music therapy, it was the therapist's intention to assist in the generalization of these behaviors:

1. To decrease the number of refusals to either comply with instructions or attempt a response in the classroom, and
2. To increase the amount of time spent actively engaged in written work without crying or yelling.

Long-term objectives included:

1. Elimination of crying and other emotional outbursts when confronted with a difficult task, and
2. An increase in risk-taking in the form of attempts at completing difficult material.

Assessment Procedures:

Target Behavior A: Refusal to comply or attempt.

Response Definition: 1) A voluntary cessation of activity before the directed behavior was completed or 2) an absence of the directed behavior. The response may or may not be accompanied by a statement such as "I can't," "No," or "I won't." Any interruption in the activity due to an outside source was not considered a refusal. The frequency of refusals was only recorded after the therapist offered a clear statement of expectation e.g., "Strum three times," "Play the G chord," or "Play this line of the song." The percentage of refusals out of total requests was calculated and graphed.

Target Behavior B: Playing the guitar appropriately.

Response Definition: Time spent fingering a chord, strumming or following instructions by responding on the guitar in a generally appropriate manner. Hitting, dropping or lifting the guitar will not be considered appropriate unless specifically called for. Playing guitar while the therapist is demonstrating or requiring other activity is also not considered appropriate. The number of seconds engaged in appropriate guitar playing was counted via a stopwatch (duration recording).

Assessment Results: As shown in Figures 11.3 and 11.4, baseline data reflect a low level of time spent playing guitar, and a high percentage of refusals. Alan held the guitar for only a short time before stating, "This is too hard for me." On the first day of observation, he left the group soon after it began, despite the therapist's gentle coaxing.

Treatment Procedures:

Antecedents: To set the occasion for successful attempts at guitar playing, the music therapist gave very simple instructions to perform on the guitar and included activities which seemed to generate the most fun. The therapist watched Alan with the guitar prior to the start of the session, and asked the group to do those movements or strums that Alan was able to do. The group was asked to imitate Alan as he would pluck a string and the rest of the group was to pluck the same string on their guitar. The group made up songs to the melody of individual strings, and paired someone strumming with another student fingering a simple chord. A nearly errorless learning environment, with step-by-step expectations, was designed for guitar instruction.

Consequences: Contrary to his behavior during lessons, Alan enjoyed experimenting with the guitar when he was alone. As a special privilege, Alan was allowed to spend some of his elective time after lunch practicing on his own. A specific contingent relationship was developed between time spent playing guitar during his lessons and time allowed for free practice. For each minute Alan participated by playing guitar during the lesson, he earned the same number of minutes of practice time on that day. The therapist also made sure that Alan received positive feedback for any progress made.

Techniques: The music therapist provided as many opportunities for success as possible. Praise was given plentifully for an approximation of the desired response. To ensure some consistency in data collection, the therapist attempted to devote equal time to instruction or modeling and the student's imitation or playing as requested. In this way, approximately 15 minutes of appropriate guitar playing was possible.

Music Techniques: Guitar instruction started with games in which students experimented with different sounds, then imitated plucking single strings, and strummed across open strings. Simple fingerings were introduced, e.g., G chord with top four strings only, requiring one finger. Several songs were sung with the one chord. When the D^7 chord was taught, two students played only the G chord while two others played the D^7 on cue. Together, the ensemble accompanied a great number of popular tunes without changing fingering. A lesson on notation was phased in. Later, changing chords, new simple chords and standard fingerings were demonstrated as new songs were learned.

Generalization Techniques:
Alan's teacher identified a set of classroom assignments which Alan refused to attempt in the past. As an incentive, when Alan completed the work, he was given the privilege of playing guitar during elective time on that day.

Another generalization strategy was the use of extensive praise from multiple sources whenever Alan attempted a new or difficult task. Teachers and family members were encouraged to comment on other benefits of this action to Alan.

Evaluation:
Because the guitar practice contingency was being implemented in the music therapy setting and the classroom, a multiple baseline design across settings was a fitting structure to test its effectiveness.

In order to examine the overall impact of music therapy, it was important to poll the teacher, parents and others with whom Alan was in close contact. Interviews of these people at the end of six months focused on their observations of the target behavior and of general functioning.

Figure 11.3 represents a multiple baseline design across the two settings for on-task behavior. It should be noted that Alan soon learned that he could merely fill up the pages of his workbook in class and earn the reward. At this time, the teacher changed the criterion such that it was clear that Alan was trying his best. Time on-task to those assignments was recorded on a daily basis. She watched Alan to determine whether he was spending time on each problem or question, actively engaged in looking at his paper, writing, or looking up as if thinking, but not visually focusing on someone in the room.

Figures 11.3 and 11.4 demonstrate a successful change in behavior. With some exceptions on days in which Alan gave up due to some new challenges on the guitar, he stayed with the group during most all of the lessons. Reports from parents and teacher are more revealing, however, in examining overall success. Parents noticed what they report as an immediate change in Alan. When he was alone, he often sang his new songs, and when they commented on his lovely singing voice, he seemed embarrassed, but proud. He took on a more cheerful disposition, especially when he was singing. He delighted his parents by asking for a guitar; he had never shown much interest in anything before. The teacher believed the guitar to be a tremendous expressive outlet for Alan, and it was obviously something for which he would work very hard. The school psychologist, likewise, observed great personality changes in Alan during that year. He was more open, less apt to become emotional, and much more willing to try new things. The IEP team actually recommended mainstreaming Alan back into the regular classroom in the following academic year. Although these changes may have been developmental or due to any number of environmental factors, it is likely that music therapy played a part in these results.

Results:

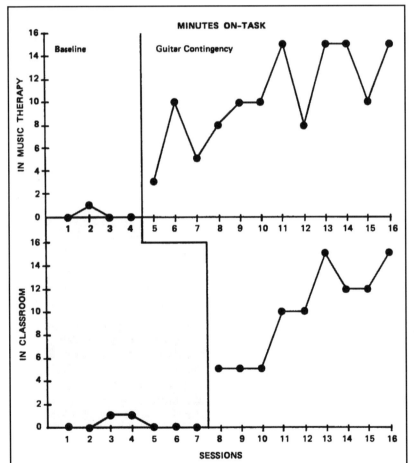

Figure 11.3. Alan's on-task behavior in music therapy and classroom.

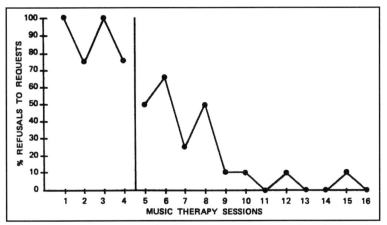

Figure 11.4. Percentage of refusals by Alan during baseline and music therapy.

At the end of the six months, the music therapist located a used guitar at a price affordable to Alan's family, organized an after-school folk/rock guitar group, and recommended private lessons by someone in the community. Follow-up data reveal that Alan has adjusted well to the regular classroom and continues to enjoy guitar lessons.

Music Therapy in a Correctional Facility

Clientele and Setting:
Inmates of a State Correctional Facility for Women were given the opportunity to attend music therapy twice a week. A group of women who were anticipating release from the facility within the following year were given the choice of participating in a vocational training program or music therapy. Twelve elected music therapy and fifteen chose the vocational program.

Objectives:
The primary objective was to increase self-esteem.

Assessment Procedures:
Target Behavior: Self-esteem
    Response Definition: Self-esteem was operationally defined as responses on a Self-Esteem Inventory adapted from available standardized tests of self-esteem.

Assessment Results: Self-esteem was measured in all 27 women at the beginning of the music therapy program, and two months later, before the first participant was released. Subsequently, the inventory was administered when the remaining participants of both groups left the facility.

Treatment Procedures:
Music therapy sessions were loosely structured, intended to provide a nonthreatening environment in which participants could make decisions regarding how they wished to spend their music therapy hour and the goals toward which they desired to work. The therapist functioned as a group facilitator, emphasizing the positive aspects of their interactions and intervening when she had feedback to offer. She also identified certain guidelines and options for the group to consider. After experimenting with various music experiences, songwriting, lyric analysis, and improvisation on percussion became the favored modalities for therapy.

A long-term plan was devised for the music therapist to maintain contact with these 27 women and others who subsequently joined the group. Through State Parole Officers, data were collected on offenses committed following release in the community. Some officers agreed to administer the inventories during the first year of parole, with the parolee's permission.

Results:

	Pretest		2-month Posttest		Pre-release Test		6-8 Month Posttest	
	M	SD	M	SD	M	SD	M	SD
Music	50	8.5	85	5.3	75	9.1	58	8.5
Vocational	52	7.2	55	8.5	55	9.0	40	7.9

Figure 11.5. Self-esteem scores of participants in music therapy and vocational training.

Data for the original participants are shown in Figure 11.5. Although it was not possible to obtain follow-up information on all 27, inventory results were gathered on nine music therapy participants and seven vocational trainees at all of the following times: pretest, two months later, pre-release, and six to eight months after release. One year after release, information regarding whether parole rules were broken was also available on these 16 women.

As shown in the table, self-esteem scores rose dramatically from pretest to testing two months later in the music therapy group. There was a significant difference between scores of the music therapy and vocational groups when subjected to a statistical analysis (p <.05). Although there was a drop in self-esteem at the time of release from the institution, the difference between groups was still significant, in favor of music therapy (p <.05). Six to eight months after release, self-esteem dropped, but not as low as during the pretest for the music therapy group.

Of those who were followed for one year post-release, a lower percentage of music therapy participants had parole violations, but this difference between groups was not significant.

Guards and other staff working with the participants reported that the women looked forward to the sessions with great expectation. Many women expressed that the group session gave them the first opportunity they ever had to be themselves and begin to trust others. Several thanked the music therapist for understanding them and giving them the emotional outlet of music. Others said they never realized that music could be such an important part of their lives. "It was the only time that I felt like somebody," said one young woman.

As the music therapy program at the State Correctional Facility has evolved, the group itself is now setting specific objectives and examining its own outcomes. The group has developed a set of guidelines and is far more organized than it was originally. Self-evaluation, drawing on the group's own stated objectives, would be a valuable way to determine program effectiveness in addition to giving participants more responsibility in the decision-making process. It is recommended that such evaluation strategies be explored as the music therapy program continues.

An Unsolicited Evaluation

Miko is an 85-year-old woman who is homebound due to her frailty and ill health. She was referred to the music therapist because of depression. After five months of music therapy, Miko wrote a personal note to the therapist. The following are excerpts:

"When I started music therapy, I was in a horrible state. I think I had given up on life. You know, all of my friends have died. It's my turn. But, I always loved the piano and music. You showed me that I had love again and could love the music we played.

...I never thought I would fulfill my dreams to play piano. Now, I don't sound very good. But, I am playing and I am getting better—not just on piano. There's no need to be morose. I have my piano and it lets me be whoever I want to be.

...You warned me about being alone with the piano. I'm not; I invited over my new neighbor. She plays piano very well. We have something in common—the love of music. My visiting nurse likes to listen to me. Isn't that something?

...Anyway, I don't sit in bed, dreading getting out of it. I lumber over to the piano before I brush my teeth. I can't wait! I just play my "black note songs," and every day, there is a new song!

...I don't remember having something to look forward to. Somehow, there really is something to live for. I love the music. Just like you said, maybe it is okay to love myself and my new self, too!"

Analysis of Clinical Examples

Note the variation in the four examples. The first, a program for stress reduction, is detailed in regard to the quantitative results of body tension observations and questionnaire responses. The experimental design entailed numerous controls, using the jargon of scientific methodology. The individual study of a child with a behavioral disorder was more precise in describing the target behaviors of the child. Graphic presentations of results yielded a discussion of numerous areas of change over the course of music therapy. The third example, a correctional program, was less detailed than the other two. Working with a very flexible design and a large changing clientele, the therapist reported in a less formal manner. The fourth case was an unsolicited personal evaluation. This woman was able to articulate her insights and her transformation which came about through self-examination.

These evaluations meet the requirements of distinctly different clinical environments. They demonstrate the diversity of formats for a final music therapy evaluation. They also show the variety of perspectives that contribute to the evaluation process.

Summary

Defining success is prerequisite to determining whether it has been accomplished. The final evaluation reports the degree of success or failure of music therapy to reach the therapeutic goal. This chapter describes the importance of documenting other outcomes and making recommendations for the future. Results are communicated with the audience in mind. Four examples of clinical reports deal with: reducing stress in business people, teaching guitar to a child with a behavioral disorder, music therapy in a correctional facility, and a self-evaluation by an 85-year-old woman. The examples illustrate the variation in style of presentation possible in an effective final evaluation.

Key Words

Secondary gains
   Unexpected and unplanned outcomes over the
   course of therapy.

For Further Reading

APA Commission on Psychotherapies. (1982).
   *Psychotherapy research: Methodological and effi-
   cacy issues*. Washington, DC: American Psychiatric
   Association.
Hanser, S. B. (1980). *Music therapy practicum: A
   manual for behavioral change through music
   therapy*. Oakland, CA: Pea Press.

Music is an outburst of the soul.
—*Frederick Delius (1862–1934)*

Chapter **12**

Termination

When I think of termination in my life, I think of loss, separation, withdrawal, isolation, and a sense of "never again" or "no more." Endings are as plentiful as beginnings. Yet, it is difficult for me to reframe this part of life to mean completion, fulfillment, achievement, and a positive, natural aspect of the life cycle. As with most of us, I have lost loved ones and experienced the split of significant relationships. Hence, when it is time to terminate professional relationships in the music therapy sessions I lead, I carry these associations with me.

As a music therapist, I deal with closure as an important part of every session. The need to end one thing before starting another is a recognized, recurring life theme. Colloquial psychology has coined "unfinished business" as a concept requiring completion before an individual can move on to a new relationship, decision, or direction.

The human tendency is to avoid termination or at least, to bring our own history and biases to it. This challenges therapists to consider how we can facilitate this stage of therapy to ensure that the client's needs are being served while we process our own perspectives on termination. This chapter presents some considerations for transforming this last stage of therapy into a valuable set of lessons for the person and therapist.

Guidelines for Termination

Should Music Therapy Be Terminated?

The fulfillment of musical potential is a lifelong process. Many have claimed that the achievement of true awareness is in the seeking. Self-actualization is an ideal that we strive to know and experience. If these are the therapeutic goals, then music therapy could continue indefinitely. After all, there is always more to gain and more to experience.

On the other hand, the professional service of music therapy is performed for a specific function to address an expressed need. If music therapy is provided for a lofty long-term goal, there is still the therapeutic relationship to consider. After working together for a lengthy period of time, would the person benefit from working with another therapist who offers a different area of expertise or a distinctive approach to the problem?

When the therapist looks inward to examine personal motivation, is there a bias toward continuing therapy to meet the therapist's needs? The therapist must identify the countertransference or projection that may accompany the therapeutic alliance. If there are associations to one's own life generated by this impending change, they should be processed within supervision or other outside venue. There are obvious circumstances, such as the income generated by continuing therapy, which contribute to a therapist's bias toward maintaining the person in therapy.

The American Music Therapy Association Standards of Practice (1998) offer direction on the subject. This document states:

"The music therapist will terminate music therapy when the client has attained stated goals and objectives, fails to benefit from services, can no longer be scheduled, or is discharged. At the time of termination, consideration will be given for scheduling periodic reassessment to determine the need for follow-up services. The music therapist will prepare the music therapy termination plan in accordance with federal, state, and facility regulations."

When Should Music Therapy Be Terminated?

The simple answer is straightforward: Terminate when the goal is reached. When music therapy is successful, however, secondary gains point to the potential of this modality to benefit the person in many other ways. The question arises: If the person could achieve this goal so successfully in music therapy, then what outcomes could be obtained by continuing this effective approach? That brings the argument for continuation full circle, with the contention that more is better. The ultimate decision rests in mutual agreement between therapist and client.

Other factors dictate termination. When the amassed data point out that there is no improvement prior to the contracted review date, this fact should be communicated to the clinical team, family or person. Often, there is an impasse in therapy where no progress is made for a period of weeks. This circumstance should be discussed openly with the client or persons responsible for the client's care. The decision regarding termination is made by the appropriate parties after examining the data and consulting the music therapist and when feasible, the client.

Sometimes, the therapeutic relationship is unhealthy. This is a matter for the therapist to bring to supervision or consultation with a fellow professional. Outside perspectives are welcome when the therapist senses that the relationship with the client is complicated or not serving the client's needs. There may be signs from the client that termination is being considered. When the person misses several appointments or arrives consistently late, this may indicate that there is a problem. Resistance is an expected factor in the course of psychotherapy, but can be an early indication that the person will be terminating therapy. This must be addressed as soon as it is observed, or the opportunity may be lost.

How Does the Music Therapist Prepare for Termination?
At the first sign that goals are being reached, or that any of the above problems exist, the music therapist must discuss the feasibility of termination with the appropriate persons. If a termination or review date is written into the contract, the therapist should bring up the subject of termination several weeks in advance.

The termination discussion should include:
    1. an evaluation of therapy and the person's progress;

2. a date for the last session;

3. a plan for phasing out sessions, if feasible;

4. recognition of the feelings associated with termination; and

5. a focus on the person's future, including recommendations for other services and plans for reassessment or follow-up.

Sharing the data regarding progress is important to help the person or significant others understand the changes that took place during therapy. It is important to consider the person's or family's feedback about areas of skill transfer and impressions of therapeutic impact.

The date for the final session should be mutually agreeable and far enough in the future to prepare for the transition away from therapy. Some therapists phase out the schedule gradually, setting bi-weekly or monthly sessions. Follow-up telephone calls, meetings in the community, or a re-assessment of progress are generally articulated in the Generalization Plan.

There are several areas to investigate before therapy comes to a close. Issues of separation or abandonment may be triggered by impending termination. Another theme is loss and transition. Exploring the person's feelings and sharing personal perspectives is important to ensure a positive closure to the experience. It may be advisable to determine whether the client feels a sense of failure at termination. This is the stage of therapy in which to ask questions and disclose clinical impressions that will assist the person to process and learn while preparing to move on independently.

Reminders and reinforcement of generalization strategies are critical in ensuring that transfer takes place. Recommendations for other treatment, follow-up services, or monitoring of progress are indicated. This planning requires the cooperation of others and should be sought as early as possible in treatment planning to ensure that it is feasible when the time for termination arrives.

What Happens with an Unplanned Termination?

Often, the music therapist, student, or intern completes a contract or rotation and must terminate before goals are met. In this case, it is essential to prepare the person in the same way as in a planned termination. If another music therapist will be substituted, introducing the new therapist in the last sessions may ease the transition. Most importantly, sensitivity to the feelings that arise while making plans for the remaining work will serve all parties well.

At times, the client is transferred, moves from the area, or chooses to leave music therapy. The therapist must be careful not to project personal emotions or resentment while facilitating a healthy processing of feelings. Focusing on the future and the progress which has been achieved in therapy is especially important.

Musical Termination

Music therapists are fortunate to have a medium to process loss and endings in a fruitful and creative way. Communicating feelings through musical performance and improvisation is one of the music therapist's most effective strategies. Analyzing song lyrics about the end of an era or life transition helps individuals understand the feelings underlying upcoming termination. Comparing songs and pieces to express what music therapy has meant is another useful technique.

Recording compositions, improvisations, and performances offers the person a permanent product of music therapy experiences. Some therapists transcribe the words to songs for clients to take with them. The final session may become a ritual for transition, growth, mourning, new beginnings and other aspects of closure.

Termination becomes a celebration of accomplishments, a legacy of achievements, and the culmination of work and play in music therapy. Termination means taking new skills and behaviors practiced in music therapy, owning them, applying them, and building upon them. It is a time for congratulating the person on what he or she has brought to music therapy and given in the process. It is a time to recognize the growth that has taken place and to acknowledge the gifts of creativity that the person has shared in music therapy.

Clinical Example

The six-month internship was about to come to a close. The music therapy intern wanted to prepare the group at the Day Hospital that she would be leaving in three weeks. She told them that another intern would be taking over. She told them that she was feeling sad to be leaving the group and the hospital. She was excited about starting a new job, but had enjoyed working with the people in the group and was greatly inspired by how they had opened up and worked hard to cope with their problems. She was aware that several group members had divorced recently and wondered if the idea of her departure had brought up feelings of abandonment. She asked if she could play the Country Western song, "D-I-V-O-R-C-E." The participants listened, some of them singing along. They spoke about the lyrics. One person commented that he would miss the intern. He had a hard time after his wife left. With great emotion in his voice, he described how every transition was difficult for him. Several others empathized, discussing the feelings that surfaced as they listened to the music.

The intern asked if the group wanted to meet her successor at their next session. They did. They also suggested that they write a song about all the thoughts and feelings generated by her departure. They planned a song-writing session and a farewell sing-along of favorite songs with themes of transition and hope for their last meeting.

Summary

Termination is an important final stage of music therapy. Termination is indicated when the therapeutic goal is reached. In reality, many other factors contribute to the decision to terminate. The idea that music therapy may be a lifelong process of self-actualization is raised. It is the responsibility of the professional music therapist to terminate when goals are achieved or the client is not able to benefit from therapy. Other reasons include a lack of improvement, an impasse, and an unhealthy therapeutic relationship. The termination phase of therapy includes an evaluation of progress, a plan for the last session, a phasing out schedule, discussion of feelings surrounding termination, and a focus on the future, including recommendations and follow-up.

Music therapy is unique in having a built-in mode of celebration and ritual in its practice. Music-based termination focuses on expressing feelings, creating products of music therapy experiences, and ritualizing the transition.

References

American Music Therapy Association. (1998). *Standards of clinical practice.* Silver Spring, MD: Author.

For Further Reading

Kupers, T. A. (1988). *Ending therapy: The meaning of termination.* New York: New York University Press.

McGuire, M. G., & Smeltekop, R. A. (1994). The termination process in music therapy: Part 1 — Theory and clinical implications. *Music Therapy Perspectives. 12,* 20–27.

McGuire, M. G., & Smeltekop, R. A. (1994). The termination process in music therapy: Part 2 — A model and clinical applications. *Music Therapy Perspectives. 12,* 28–33.

Yalom, I. (1995). *The theory and practice of group psychotherapy* (4th ed.). New York: Basic Books.

Index

Author **I**ndex

About the Author

Suzanne B. Hanser, Ed.D., MT-BC chairs the Music Therapy Department at Berklee College of Music and is a lecturer in the Department of Social Medicine at Harvard Medical School. She is past president of the National Association for Music Therapy. Dr. Hanser received a National Research Services Award from the National Institute on Aging and was a Senior Postdoctoral Fellow at Stanford University School of Medicine. Dr. Hanser has served as program director of the Alzheimer's Association, San Francisco Bay Area Chapter, and Chair of the Music Therapy Department at University of the Pacific. She received her music therapy training at The Florida State University and doctoral degree from Columbia University where she was a Fellow of the Center for the Behavioral Analysis of School Learning.

Photo ©1999 Kimberly Grant

More Fine Publications from Berklee Press

As Serious About Music As You Are.

Music Technology and Method Books

from Berklee Press

As Serious About Music As You Are.

Prices and availability subject to change without notice.